SAY GOOD-BYE

T

ADD an

BY

DEVI S. NAMBUDRIPAD
D.C., L.Ac., R.N., Ph.D.

The AUTHOR OF

"SAY GOOD-BYE TO..." SERIES

"The doctor of the future will give no medicine,
But will interest his patients
In the care of the human frame, in diet,
And in the cause and prevention of disease"

Thomas A. Edison

Published
by

DELTA PUBLISHING COMPANY
6714 Beach Blvd.
Buena Park, CA 90621

(888)-890-0670, (714) 523 8900
Fax: (714)-523-3068
Web site: www.naet.com
e-mail:naet@earthlink.net

DEDICATION

**This book is dedicated to
all ADD and ADHD children of the world**

First Edition: September, 1999

Library of Congress: 98-93778

ISBN: 0-9658242-4-1

Printed in U.S.A.

CONTENTS

A Few Words from a Parent of ADHD children and an ADHD adult

I'm a chiropractor with three children with ADHD. After taking the first Basic NAET seminar, **I treated my children (who had various degrees of ADHD) for their basic ten allergies. Afterwards, all three children had no ADD or ADHD symptoms.** My family life has completely changed. **No more violent outbursts, uncontrollable weeping episodes and erratic and crazy behavior. No more** making several dishes for each meal to avoid individual allergies. My children are focused, calm, healthy and happy. So am I! **Thank you Dr. Nambudripad for discovering NAET and sharing it with me!**

Claire Sutherland, D.C.
Thousand Oaks, CA

Adult ADHD

I am 28 years old, and since the time I was 10 years old, I suffered from severe joint pains, headaches, irritability, insomnia, anger and hostility towards everyone that I came in contact with. My doctors did not know the cause of my problems. Every joint from my toe to my jaw gave me pain almost 24 hours a day. Since the pain and calming medication I was given didn't work and/or made me sick, **the doctors said I would just have to live with the pain.**

At the age of 18, with a height of 5'6" and weighing 110 lbs., I started to have problems with my stomach. No matter what I ate, I would have a terrible burning and or nauseous feeling. Soon after that, I started having problems with my bowels. The doctors could find nothing. So **the only answer was that it**

was stress from school-work or that it was all in my head. A few months later I developed a problem with my lungs. My lungs felt like they were on fire. Every shallow breath I took was accompanied with sharp pains that forced me to lie very still and often be bedridden for weeks at a time. **At 19, I was struggling to maintain 95 lbs.**

At 23, I started to display typical food allergies. **First milk then eggs, corn and wheat. After eating these foods my stomach and bowels would be upset for hours or the whole day.** This was easily taken care of by avoiding those foods or so I thought. But it wasn't easy to avoid the foods. I steadily began losing more pounds.

By the time I was 24, I could no longer hold down a job. I had begun to get migraines on a daily basis. By the age of 27, I was down to 85 lbs. That's when I was referred to Dr. Devi. After being treated through NAET for chicken and egg on my first visit, I was able to eat as many eggs as often as I wanted without any pain. Something I hadn't been able to do in 8 years. Treatment after treatment **I began to be able to have foods I could only dream about eating in the past.** Learning to test myself with Dr. Devi's ring test before I eat something has saved me from needless pain and suffering. (I am now maintaining 115 lbs.)

7 months and 40 treatments later I am 85 % better with more good days than bad. I am on my way to being 100 % well for the rest of my life!

Dr. Devi's NAET has given me a second chance to be a happy, healthy and productive human being. I have a steady job and I can eat all the food I want. Now my only problem is that I have to watch my weight!

Thank you Dr. Devi !!!

Samantha Stevenson
Fullerton, CA

ACKNOWLEDGMENTS

I am deeply grateful to my husband, Dr. Kris K. Nambudripad, for his inspiration, encouragement and assistance in my schooling and later, in the formulation of this project. Without his cooperation in researching reference work, revision of manuscripts, word processing and proofreading, it is doubtful whether this book would ever have been completed. My sincere thanks also go to the many clients who have entrusted their care to me, for without them I would have had no case studies, no technique and certainly no extensive source of personal research upon which to base this book.

I am also deeply grateful to the parents of David Karaba, Tim Jones, Timmy Watts, Kimberly, Toree Elston, Helene Singer, May Johnson, and Margaret Davies, for believing in me from the very beginning of my research, supporting my theory and helping me conduct the on-going *detective* work. I also have to express my thanks to my son, Roy, who assisted me in many ways in the writing of this book. Roy was a year old and very sick when I began my search for peace with health. He was very hyperactive as a child. I had to work very hard to try and find a way to keep him calm and focused without placing him on Ritalin, the preferred choice of treatment at that time. Now, he is an 18-year-old healthy, level headed, responsible teenager. From the beginning of my search for a cure to his problem, which is actually a problem of most modern children, I developed and continually refined my technique.

Additionally, I wish to thank Art Hunter, Janice Barone, and many of my friends who wish to remain anonymous for proofreading the work, and Mr. Sridharan at Delta Publishing for his printing expertise. I am deeply grateful for my professional training and the knowledge and skills acquired in classes and seminars on chiropractic and applied kinesiology at the Los Angeles College of Chiropractic in Whittier, California; the California Acupuncture College in Los Angeles; SAMRA University of Oriental Medicine, Los Angeles; and the clinical experience obtained at the clinics attached to these colleges.

My special thanks also go to the late Dr. Richard F. Farquhar at Farquhar Chiropractic Clinic in Bellflower, California. Under Dr. R. F. Farquhar, I accumulated many hours of special instruction and hands-on practice in kinesiology.

I extend my sincere thanks to these great teachers. They have helped me to grow immensely at all levels. My mentors are also indirectly responsible for the improvement of my personal health as well as that of my family, patients and other NAET practitioners among whom are countless doctors of western and oriental medicine, chiropractic, osteopathy, as well as their patients.

Many of the nutritionists instrumental in this process, were professors at the institutions I have mentioned. Their willingness to give of themselves to teach, as well as their commitment of personal time to give the interviews necessary to complete this work, places them beyond my mere expressions of gratitude. They are servants to the greatest ideals of the medical profession.

Devi S. Nambudripad, D.C., L.Ac., R.N., Ph.D.

FOREWORD

ADD/ADHD

Ritalin Deficiency or Allergies?

Sandra C. Denton, M.D.

*M*ore than one million American children take Ritalin regularly to help them with Attention Deficit Disorder, an increase of two and a half times since 1990. *Do we have a miracle cure—or over-medicated kids? (Newsweek, March 18, 1996, cover story). ADHD has become America's No. 1 childhood psychiatric disorder.*

It is not unusual for schools to mandate that the ADHD child be medicated in order to stay in class.

Why all the fuss? Just take a pill and everyone will be happy—teachers, parents, family, and neighbors. It is so much easier than having to alter life style by changing the diet and taking the time to track down the actual cause of the problem for the individual child.

Well, first of all, the pill doesn't work for everyone and second, even with correct doses, there may be side effects. These include sleep disturbances, stomach pains, facial tics and irritability, particularly when the dose is wearing off. Many parents report their child turns into a zombie or robot. Besides, no one knows the long-term consequences of taking this medication on our children or on their offspring. Why put an unnecessary burden on the liver and kidneys to detoxify these medications when there may be another answer to this problem that can so disrupt a family's world. An answer that doesn't just cover up the symptom but may actually treat the root cause of the problem without side effects!

Since 1985, I have found that working with ADHD children and their parents to be both challenging and very rewarding. Identifying the causes and aggravating factors of a disease or condition is the foundation for any therapy I use for my patients, no matter what "label" their disease may carry. I would say that in the early years of treating this condition, I had a success rate of about 40-50%. But since being introduced to Nambudripad's Allergy Elimination Technique (NAET), which saved my life in 1991 (see foreword to Dr. Devi's book Say Good-bye to Illness), my success rate is about 90%. Let me share some of my results with you, but you will want to read this book from cover to cover to learn for yourself more of the details.

◆ Mineral deficiencies, caused both by poor nutritional intake as well as by allergies to these minerals, are a significant contributing factor in ADHD. Statistics show that 100% of these children are deficient in magnesium, 50% are deficient in manganese, and 80%are deficient in zinc. Supplementation is much more effective after clearing the allergies by NAET.

◆ Both allergy to sugars and a high intake of sugar contribute to the hyperactive behavior in some children while causing decreased concentration and drowsiness in others. If you doubt this finding, ask why it is almost impossible to find a substitute teacher the day after Halloween. Artificial sweeteners, food additives, sulfites, MSG, food coloring and flavorings, and salicylates may need to be eliminated from the diet. Muscle Response Testing (MRT) will verify the allergies to these substances and then they can be treated by NAET.

◆ Candida /Yeast problems are found in almost all of these children. My mentor, Jonathan Wright, M.D., (Kent, Washington) used to say that chronic infections anywhere in the body were most likely caused by allergies. So it is not surprising that many ADHD patients have taken repeated doses of antibiotics, some even for months at a time, usually without any recommendation of acidophilus products — hence the perfect setup for candida. ADHD patients will not get better until you remove the sugar/yeast foods that support candida and administer anti-fungal agents along with acidophilus to restore the normal intestinal bacterial flora for at least six months. Of course, NAET treatments for candida mixture and for the specific antibiotics that were utilized will shorten the recovery time.

♦ Because antibiotics are sweetened with sugar, cavities develop in the teeth. The material commonly used for filling the teeth is mercury, a neuro-toxic, which depletes the body of the very minerals it needs, attacks the immune system aggravating allergies, and hinders every hormone in the body, along with many other adverse effects. Nickel used in braces and retainers can also alter immune and brain function. Fluoride treatments and fluoride toothpaste can be toxic to many people by disrupting enzyme systems. Popular toothpaste may contain sugar, food coloring, and cornstarch. The health practitioner may need to NAET these dental items along with many combinations. I remember one case in particular, which demonstrates this point. The parents brought their child to me in desperation for nutritional counseling. Up until that year he had been a top performer. Now he had to be placed in a special education class because he could not keep up with his studies or stay focused for more than two or three minutes at a time. The parents had been required to see psychiatrists because the school administrators and his general practitioner felt that there must be something wrong with them that was causing the boy's difficulties. A standard question in my history intake includes "What is in the mouth? Has he had any dental work recently?" Both parents looked at each other in surprise as they remembered that that summer he had had his first two mercury fillings placed. Because of my years of experience in this field I insisted those fillings be removed immediately. Within two weeks his performance was back where it had formerly been!

♦ Allergies to many foods, vitamins (especially B's), minerals, inhalants, mold, chemicals, parasites, insect mix, school-room air or bedroom air, pets and a host of other items need to be identified and treated. Allergies to wheat and grains, dairy, corn products, chocolate, cinnamon and peanut butter are among the most frequently seen food allergies. A child with severe dyslexia found her symptoms totally resolved after being treated by NAET for sugar, wheat/gluten, and dairy. Benjamin's parents were getting pretty frustrated with him. He was being home-schooled and within a short time of beginning his lessons, he would get sleepy, yawn, his mind would wander, and he would be unable to complete the assignment. Finally his parents would give up. He would then go play. Immediately his energy returned and he was smiling with no evidence of his previous difficulty. His parents thought surely he was just lazy and rebellious and didn't want to do school work. By MRT it was determined that he was highly allergic to the newspaper ink in his textbooks. Two days after NAET treatment, Benjamin finished his daily lesson by 11:00 a.m. to the amazement and delight of his parents. Now he has become an avid reader and is doing well with his schoolwork.

♦ Of special interest is the fact that I have not seen a single child who had ADHD that did not need to have NAET to DPT, and several cases seem to begin around the time of their booster injections prior to entering school. Sometimes other immunizations need NAET treatments such as MMR or polio. If one has already received allergy shots for any length of time, check by muscle response testing allergy to phenol or glycerin, and if positive, proceed with NAET.

♦ Many of these children have "normal" thyroid blood tests, but low temperatures and periods of unusual fatigue, dry skin, constipation and other symptoms, which suggest that a "therapeutic trial of natural thyroid" might be beneficial. Needless to say, NAET to thyroid and other hormones may be indicated.

♦ Essential fatty acid deficiency is quite common in ADHD patients and often requires NAET followed by supplementation.

♦ Hair analysis may reveal the presence of heavy metals such as cadmium, copper, lead, or aluminum. It is well known that these heavy metals are toxic and definitely alter brain performance, intellectual abilities and behavior. Blood tests are not sensitive enough; however, MRT has been useful in my practice. NAET followed by chelating these metals from the body can restore normal function and remove poisons that damage the nervous system.

♦ Allergies to neurotransmitters must be identified and treated, including GABA (often associated in hyperactivity), serotonin (sleep problems and depression), dopamine, epinephrine, norepinephrine and histamine. Any time there is an allergic reaction in the body, special cells (mast cells) release histamine. If one happens to be allergic to histamine, then a vicious cycle is begun releasing more and more histamine and then giving Benadryl or some other "anti-histamine." Vitamin C is natural anti-histamine, that is, if you are not allergic to it. It is so much easier to simply NAET histamine.

NAET is truly awesome. You will want to pass this book on to others and spread the word about this amazing technique. Anyone who has wrestled with a rotation diet or tried to eliminate wheat, sugar and dairy from a small child's diet knows what a struggle that can be. No wonder many have been so frustrated trying to manage all of these parameters that they finally resorted to giving "vitamin R." But with the NAET process all of this becomes unnecessary. An allergen can be *eliminated* within 25 hours of treatment! No more having to avoid the food or give up a beloved pet.

NAET can save a child from the stigma of being "different" and enable the child to maximize his education and reach his highest potential. Even if a person has made it to adulthood and suffers from ADD, there is still hope. It is never too late to seek help and begin to make changes. No longer does ADD have to dictate what kind of job you can handle or continue to damage your self-confidence. By finding a NAET practitioner in your area, and following through with the treatments, you can get a new lease on life and tackle new horizons.

Sometimes people quit after only 4 or 5 treatments because they think it is too hard or taking too long. I can only encourage them to persevere and not give up. While it may take a lot of work identifying and clearing the allergens one by one, many patients have succeeded in becoming "free at last" from their allergies and able to lead normal lives!

Sandra C. Denton, M.D.
Alaska Alternative Medicine Center
3201 C St. #602
Anchorage, AK.99503
907-563-6200

PREFACE

Since childhood I suffered from a multitude of health problems. As an infant, I had severe infantile eczema,which lasted until I was seven or eight years old. I was given western medicine and Ayurvedic herbal medicine without a break. When I was eight years old, one of the herbal doctors told my parents to feed me white rice cooked with a special herb formula. This special diet helped me a great deal. The herbalist seemed to know what he was doing. But it didn't cure my problem. It only gave temporary relief until I discovered NAET.

In 1976, I relocated to Los Angeles. I became more health-conscious and tried to change my eating habits adding more whole grain products and complex carbohydrates. All of a sudden, I became very ill. I suffered from bronchitis, pneumonia and my arthritis returned. My symptoms multiplied. I suffered from insomnia, clinical depression, constant sinusitis and frequent migraine headaches. I felt extremely tired all the time, but I remained wide-awake when I went to bed. I tried many different antibiotics and medicines, changed doctors and consulted nutritionists. All the medications, vitamins and herbs made me sicker, and the consumption of good nutrition made me worse. I was nauseated all the time. Every inch of my body ached. I lived on aspirin, taking almost 30 aspirin a day to keep me going.

During this time, I had three miscarriages, which affected me emotionally. For the fourth time I again conceived. This time I suffered from severe morning sickness. I couldn't lift my head due to severe headaches. I couldn't keep any food inside my stomach. I threw up every time I put any food in my mouth. I lived on saltine crackers, cottage cheese and water. I vomitted at least 15-20 times a day. Finally, my doctor put me on Bendectin 1X3 day for two months. I felt better on Bendectin. I was able to function somewhat better. But after the fourth month, when I continued to vomit, he refused to give me Bendectin saying that it could cause anomalies in the growing fetus. My morning sickness returned stronger than before. Reluctantly, he prescribed the Bendectin for me after I signed a release that if my baby becomes deformed, I won't hold him responsible.

I took Bendectin until the day I went to the hospital to have my baby. It was a life saver for me. Everything else went fine this time and my baby was born — a healthy looking 8 pound handsome boy! His skin was soft like a rose petal. When the nurse placed him in my arms just few hours after his birth, he looked at me with his eyes wide open and I thought he smiled at me. He looked gorgeous!

But on the second day, when the nurse brought him all wrapped up in his baby blanket, and placed the bundle in my arms, I took one look at his face and I let out a painful cry. The flowery-soft skin of his face was replaced with huge red hives and his body was covered with red miliary rashes. He was irritable and cried non-stop. The nurse thought if I nursed him he might calm down.

He cried until he was tired. Nothing gave him any relief. On the fifth day, I left the hospital with a bunch of skin cream and a baby that was covered with red, irritated and peeling skin from head to toe.

Even at home he cried most of the time. He suffered from severe constipation and flatulence. He continued to have rashes all over his body. He suffered from severe insomnia. He cried almost 20 hours a day. I had to put him in the baby seat and my husband and I drove long distances on the free ways aimlessly just to make him sleep a few hours. While he was in the moving car he slept. As soon as the car stopped, he would wake up crying. So he cried almost all day. At the night he slept for a few hours during our drive. This became a routine. I couldn't sleep the whole night either. How could I sleep when he was crying? I would look at my son's helpless face and hug him tightly saying "we worked very hard to get you my son, please be healthy. I can't see you sick like this." Then I would pray, "God, please make my son healthy...I won't ask anything else from you in this life again."

Finally, my mother came to help me. In tears, I told her my predicament. The infant won't stop crying. I told her that I tried every trick that I learned from nursing school to calm a child. Nothing seemed to do any good.

She looked at the baby for a few seconds. First thing she did was take off his clothes and lay him on the cold marbled-floor. To my amazement, in just a few seconds, he was fast asleep. The next few months my mother took care of him. She put minimal clothes on him. She donated all the dozens of baby formulae to the children's hospital. She made her own special baby food from cream of rice, milk, clarified butter and raw sugar to taste. My breast mik dried up in less than a month. So, he had to depend on top feed. On my mother's special diet, he had less health problems.

One of the health problems was the repeated vomiting he had after each big meal. His pediatrician suggested a minor surgery to tighten his cardiac end of the esophagus to prevent reflex vomiting. I refused to consent for the surgery. I told the doctor, that I would consent to the surgery after he turned two. I would manage somehow until then. I couldn't bear seeing him get cut. I cried day and night, again praying to my God— my salvation for some help!

But by the time he turned one, God heard my prayers. I was enrolled in Los Angeles College of Chiropractic, learning kinesiology and muscle response testing for allergies. Through MRT, I also discovered that he was allergic to all foods, including baby formulae, baby foods, etc. He was not allergic to cream of rice and non-fat milk, which explained why he did well on my mother's special diet. He was allergic to sugar.

While I was on a diet of white rice and broccoli, he was fed on cream of rice, non-fat dry milk, and filtered water. He was allergic to vitamin-mineral supplements. I couldn't give him any vitamins. But to my surprise for the first time in months, his skin cleared up and he even began sleeping a few hours at night. The new food suited him just the way my new diet gave me energy.

But as he was growing up I saw him becoming restless and hyperactive. By the time he was four, he became very noisy and restless. I tried to put him in pre-school. The school refused to admit him unless I placed him on calming drugs. I changed four pre-schools in four months. Every one refused to take him unless I put him on 'Vitamin R' (Ritalin), which I refused to do.

So, we (my husband and I) kept him at home trying to teach him whatever we could. He couldn't understand me. He couldn't focus even for a few seconds. He jumped around restlessly and made much noise. He only spoke a few words even at four.

I was researching books and publications trying to find an answer to help my son. I knew that he was very intelligent. But his mind was very restless. He had no attention span. He could not be quiet for a few minutes. Something made him very restless. I didn't want to put him on any drugs. My mind kept saying there is a way out, don't give up. I will find the answer soon. But how? *Search...you shall find.*

Then as God-sent, I met Dr. Farquhar, D.C. He taught me various techniques from kinesiology to balance the brain and body - the techniques no one taught in the schools. I was fortunate to have met him. He changed my perspective about life.

I used all his techniques on my son. I saw the difference in his behavior. He became calmer. Whenever he got restless and uncontrollable, I would use the brain balancing techniques. He would calm down. But after months of work, I did not see any permanent change. If I wanted to keep him calm I had to do the balancing technique a number of times during the day. As a student, mother, wife, housekeeper and cook, I found this exhausting. I was pushing myself to the limit to get through each day. I didn't want to give up school; but I couldn't treat him as often as needed. I prayed that I would find a better answer soon.

And I found it! I discovered NAET!

While I was a student of oriental medicine, while I was attending one of the courses in electromagnetic energy and its interference with the human body and other surrounding objects, I arrived at a discovery, which resulted in the foundation of my own good health and my child's. The integration of the relevant techniques from the various fields I studied, combined with my own discoveries, has since become the focus of my life to help my family and me. We were an allergic family —father-mother-son! We were allergic to everything around us. There was no known successful method of treatment for food allergies then (actually even now as I am writing this), using western medicine except avoidance, which means deprivation and frustration. Each of the disciplines I studied provided bits of knowledge, which I used to develop a new allergy treatment called Nambudripad's Allergy Elimination Techniques or NAET for short.

I began treating him for his food and environmental allergies one by one. Deep in my heart, I knew that someday he was going to be okay.

After I treated him for a few food and vitamin allergies, I treated him for clothes, chemicals, environmental allergens, and his toys, etc. Then I treated his allergy towards me and mine towards him. That turned a cornerstone. He began calming down. His focus became better. His restlessness diminished. I was even able to teach him a few things. His allergies were under control soon after that.

Finally, St. Paul of the Cross school admitted him to 2nd grade. He was still hyperactive. I had treated him for B complex and sugars. They didn't seem to make much difference in his hyperactive behavior. He was still having problems with eating. So I was supplementing him with B vitamins. In the morning I would take three pills and put them in three compartments of his pill box for him to take during the day. One day he took all three pills at once. I got scared. I didn't know what was going to happen. I tried to make him vomit. This time he couldn't vomit. I was all ready to take him to the hospital.

By the time my husband returned home from work. I told him that he had eaten three B complex pills at one time. Kris said not to worry and nothing bad would happen by taking that many pills. If at all, he might get a niacin flush. Nothing else. So, I waited and watched him. To my amazement, he looked calm and sat quietly on my lap for an hour for the first time in his life. He had no adverse reaction. We sat and watched a whole movie.

The next morning I saw that he was still calm. I evaluated his activities and events of the previous day. I was looking for a reason that brought on the sudden behavior change. The only unusual thing that happened was the overdose of vitamin B complex.

Suddenly I realized that he was very deficient in vitamin B complex. "Of course, it is a nerve food!" I said to myself, "he is hyper and his body is restless due to lack of nerve-food—- B complex!" I gave him three more pills. It worked again. Next day I counted the deficiency of his B complex pills — he was deficient 3000 pills that day! I began giving him 6 pills (50 mgs each) daily. In less than 3 days, he became calm without doing any brain-balancing. I continued to give him 6 pills daily for a year. Then I reduced the dosage to three pills a day. He became very quiet and focused. He began showing interest in studies. He didn't have attention deficit disorder (ADD) or attention deficit-hyperactive disorder (ADHD) anymore. His ADHD was allergy based and nutrition deficient. When his allergies were eliminated, when his nutrient requirement was fulfilled, his brain began functioning normally like all other normal children.

He began doing well in school. What a relief! He graduated last year with 4.6 GPA from St. Paul High School at the age of 18. Thank you God, for being there for me to guide me all along!

The more extensively I studied the subject of allergies, the more I found it to be a truly fascinating, yet highly complex field. Although food allergies as causes for multiple physiological problems have been gaining acceptance as a separate area of medical study in the last few years, it certainly has not been given the recognition it deserves. In fact, knowledge of the field is still quite limited not only among the general public, but also among those who treat allergies because of the limited volume of research conducted.

After learning about the prevalence of allergies in children with ADHD and gathering a great deal of clinical hands-on experience with my son and hundreds of my young patients from my 15 years of practice as an allergist, I felt motivated to write this book on allergy-based ADHD and how to conquer it with NAET.

When I realized that most health disorders are allergy-based, my urge to inform and educate people grew. In the meantime, many of my patients and my friends insisted that I put this valuable information in book form. The best form of education is through published materials. Consequently, this book on "Say Good-bye to ADD and ADHD" came into shape.

In this book, I do use some specialized terminology, which may give some lay readers a harder time and diminish their reading pleasure and understanding. But rest assured, technical terms are kept to a minimum.

Caution has also been exercised in determining the depth of the subject matter. For instance, the way allergies and the nervous system are inextricably interrelated is just now being understood. But since the human nervous system is one of the most complex areas of human anatomy and remains largely uncharted, I decided to deal with it in a sweeping fashion, drawing the reader's attention only to the close link between the nervous system and allergic reactions.

I would feel gratified, indeed, if the up-to-date material compiled in this book were to contribute to the well-being of all ADD and ADHD children, and give their worried and frustrated parents a little peace of mind, and my dream would be fulfilled. If this book could help the tired and frustrated mothers of ADHD children, if this could help to reach NAET to the mis-diagnosed and wrongly treated ADHD children who are not ADHD in reality and help them select the right path and bring them out as calm, responsible, smart individuals, my job is done.

To enhance your understanding of the subject matter, you should check out some of the other relevant books and articles quoted as a part of this book. You will find them under the section marked "BIBLIOGRAPHY" at the conclusion of this book.

Since the main focus of this presentation is acupuncture an understanding of that medical system and an introduction to the basis of Traditional Chinese Medicine (TCM) is mandatory. You should keep in mind, however, that an in-depth introduction to oriental medicine was neither intended nor considered appropriate within the scope of this publication. Therefore I urge you to refer to appropriate books for more information on this topic. Some of the references are listed in the bibliography.

Stay Allergy-Free and Enjoy Better HEALTH!

Dr. Devi S. Nambudripad,
D.C., L.Ac., R.N., Ph.D. (Acu)
Los Angeles, California
September, 1999

CHAPTER ONE

ADHD?   WHO?   MY CHILD?

1

ADHD? WHO? MY CHILD?

NO, MY CHILD CAN'T SUFFER FROM ADHD!

It was David's first day of school. His mother was apprehensive. The kindergarten teacher was smiling as she introduced herself. David's mother felt relieved. She waved good-bye to her son and went home.

Two hours later the phone rang. The school was calling. "Please come to school immediately," the secretary said. She quickly drove to the school. David was in the principal's office kicking and screaming. It was just what his mother feared. He was unable to sit on the rug with the other children without rolling, crawling, pushing, and hitting anything or anyone near him. The teacher had tried everything to calm him down, but he was uncontrollable. In her attempt to get him off the other children sitting near him, she bent over to pick him up. David grabbed her leg and bit it. The classroom of four and five year olds was in chaos. The principal was called and David was taken to her office. After meeting with the teacher, the school counselor, the assistant principal and the principal, it was decided that David was not ready for kindergarten. He was too immature to be in such a structured setting. His mother agreed and took David home. They assured her that by next year he would be ready for school.

The following year David entered school, but he hadn't matured. He was easily distracted with a short attention span, making listening to a story difficult and learning to count almost impossible. The teacher couldn't keep him still for a minute at a time. She tried rewards, M&M's, stickers, behavior modification, time-out, but nothing worked. In the first grade the school psychologist tested him and diagnosed him as having Attention Deficit Hyperactive Disorder.

After many credible diagnostic tests and evaluations, when your doctor finally drops the bomb-shell, "Your child has Attention-Deficit Hyperactive Disorder," most parents go into a denial phase. Most mothers react by saying: "Oh, no, it can't be true! I have heard that hyperactive children are uncontrollable, irrational and totally wild. My son is a sweetheart most of the time. Occasionally he gets very active, upset and has a temper tantrum. Then of course, he is a boy. He is not going to sit quietly like a girl. Nowadays, school teachers are lazy. They don't want to do any work. They just don't want to take care of a small child. Instead, they refer an active child to doctors! The doctors have a relationship with the drug companies. So they make up reasons to push expensive pills on the poor child! Parents are thrown in the middle of the circle between the teacher-doctor-drug company. If the child doesn't take the pills, he cannot attend the school. His human right is being denied here! But how can a simple parent like me stand up against the major powers like the teacher, doctor and the drug company? "

Most fathers are devastated by the news. A father somehow thinks that his son will take after him; so, he feels responsible for his child's illness. Many questions flood his mind. Does that mean that he was hyperactive as a child? Did his son inherit it from him? "No, way. It can't be true. I wasn't hyperactive even though my parents were told that I was hyperactive by my teachers, doctors and school psychologist while I was growing up. They all were wrong. Didn't I prove that they were wrong? Didn't I complete my schooling? Don't I hold a stable secure job? Don't I take care of my family to the best of my ability? My son can't be hyperactive. He is just getting a rough deal for being a BOY! That's all."

Attention Deficit Hyperactive Disorder

What is ADHD? Has anyone heard of it before? Why did it pop up so suddenly? Is it another 21st century pop culture illness or a serious, debilitating problem?

Attention Deficit Hyperactive Disorder or ADHD, also known as Attention Deficit Disorder, is not a new disease. In fact, it is not a disease at all. ADD is a neurologically or neuro-biologically based environmentally dependent, developmental disability, estimated to affect between three to five percent of the school-age population (Professional Group for Attention Deficit Disorders, 1991).

> References to attention deficit disorder like symptoms have appeared in the medical literature for almost 100 years. In fact, this syndrome is one of the most thoroughly researched of all childhood disorders. According to scientific experts and any parent whose child has struggled with the problem, ADD is a disability that can cause serious life-long problems if it is left untreated.

In recent times, ADD has officially been dubbed Attention Deficit Hyperactivity Disorder, or ADHD (American Psychiatric Association, 1994). But to most people the name ADD still remains the more familiar term.

According to western medical researchers, the actual cause of ADHD is not known. Scientific evidence suggests that in many cases, the disorder is genetically transmitted, and results from a chemical imbalance, food allergies, or deficiency of nutrients in certain neurotransmitters. These neurotransmitters are chemicals that help the brain regulate behavior.

A study conducted by the National Institute of Mental Health showed that the rate at which the brain uses glucose, its main energy source, is lower in subjects with ADHD than in subjects without ADHD (Zametkin et al. 1990).

Children who had difficulty learning or paying attention before the 1940's were considered emotionally disturbed, mentally retarded, or culturally disadvantaged. Studies done in the 1940's identified a fourth group of children who had difficulty because of the way their nervous systems worked. Their problems were neurological in origin. These children had difficulty in school, were hyperactive, impulsive, had short attention spans and emotional problems. The term used to identify them was Minimal Brain Disorder.

> According to the 1998 statement by the National Institutes of Health, an estimated 3% to 5% of school age children are still suffering from ADHD, making it the most commonly diagnosed behavioral disorder of childhood.

After the 1940's, separate studies focused on neurological differences in the brain that caused problems in behavior and learning in school. These studies identified and named the primary areas of skill difficulty: Dyslexia for reading problems, Dysgraphia for writing problems, and Dyscalculia for math problems. Later on the term Learning Disability was applied to the types of difficulties that underlie skill problems. Between 10-20-percent of all school-aged children have learning disabilities; 20-25 percent of those children will also have attention deficit disorders and attention deficit and hyperactive disorders. Learning disability and

ADHD are two separate problems; however, they appear together so frequently that they can be considered together.

According to the statistics by the Professional Group for Attention Deficit Disorders, the percentage of children who suffer from ADHD hasn't changed much from the previous study in 1999. Even with all the increasing chemical contamination, the percentage of ADHD children remains the same. This is because more and more parents are becoming aware of the problem earlier than the school age, and seek the appropriate help sooner.

Through the 1990s, diagnosis of ADHD has accelerated rapidly, with enormous numbers of children increasingly being treated with stimulant medications, including Ritalin, Dexedrine, Adderall, and Cylert. Stimulants work by affecting areas of the brain that support attention and organization.

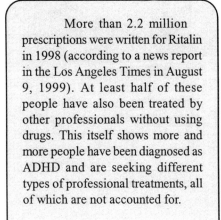

More than 2.2 million prescriptions were written for Ritalin in 1998 (according to a news report in the Los Angeles Times in August 9, 1999). At least half of these people have also been treated by other professionals without using drugs. This itself shows more and more people have been diagnosed as ADHD and are seeking different types of professional treatments, all of which are not accounted for.

Hyperactivity, distractibility, and impulsivity were initially called Hyperkinetic Disorder of Childhood (Hyperactive child). In the 1980's the name changed to Attention Deficit Disorder (ADD), to emphasize that the attention problem was the major issue, not hyperactivity. In 1987, the term was changed to Attention Deficit Hyperactivity Disorder (ADHD).

Learning disabilities can occur in any of the four areas of the brain used in the learning process: recording information (input), organizing and understanding (integration), storing for later use (memory), and communicating (output). The most common learning disability in ADHD children is an auditory processing deficit (difficulty remembering verbal directions). The focus of this book will emphasize how to eliminate ADHD symptoms and behaviors rather than examining the disabilities that occur in sequencing, abstraction, organization, memory, language, and motor skills.

Attention Deficit Disorder, ADD, ADHD, or hyperactivity occurs in young children, most of them males (80% of boys and 50% of girls are hyperactive). A normal attention span is 3 to 5 minutes for each year of a child's age. A three-year-old should be able to concentrate on a particular task for at least 9 minutes; a child in kindergarten should be able to concentrate for at least 15 minutes. (Sitting in front of the television is not an accurate account of a child's attention span).

Children, who haven't learned to listen when someone talks, wait their turn, complete a task, or return to a task if interrupted, have the characteristics of ADHD. These are normal actions of children less than three or four years old.

ADHD was thought to be exclusively a childhood disease that required only temporary medication. But, the latest research has shown that 50% of children with ADHD may carry the disorder into adulthood.

Three types of behaviors characterize children or adults with ADHD. They may show one or all of these characteristics. Only one is necessary to be diagnosed as ADHD. For example, a person may be impulsive and distractible, but not hyperactive or may be just hyperactive. Everyone at some time in life is distractible, impulsive or hyperactive; however, if these behaviors are chronic throughout the person's life and present every day, he/she may be identified as having ADHD.

Children with attention deficit hyperactive disorder usually have a lot of trouble paying attention, concentrating on tasks, and are easily distracted. These children often are impulsive. There are two branches of this disorder: one group of children has difficulty paying attention (attention deficit disorder or ADD) and are not excessively active; the other group suffers from attention deficit, but they are also hyperkinetic, fidgety, impulsive and restless, and are known as ADHD or attention deficit hyperactive.

WHAT IS HYPERACTIVITY?

Hyperactive children appear to be in constant motion: running, jumping, climbing, rocking, rolling, wiggling, and jiggling. Their fingers will tap, and their legs will swing, or their body will move while sitting in a chair. Mealtime can become difficult because these children may be up and down, out of their seat, tossing food around, tapping the utensils on the table, and playing with the food. In a structured setting like school, these children may have discipline problems because of their inability to keep still.

WHAT IS DISTRACTIBILTY ?

Everyday the brain is bombarded with information from different sensory stimulators. The lower level of the brain monitors this input and relays only the important information to the thinking part of the brain. The mind would be extremely cluttered with information without this ability to sort things out. You can be in a noisy room and still have a conversation or do work while music is playing on the radio. People with ADHD have difficulty filtering out unnecessary inputs, are easily distracted, and have a short attention span.

WHAT IS IMPULSIVITY?

Children with ADHD seem to act before thinking. They answer the teacher's questions before the teacher finishes asking. They may get angry and yell, throw or hit. These children do not learn from experience because they cannot stop long enough to reflect before acting. As a result ADHD children get into behavioral difficulties at home, in school, and with friends.

Frustration, failure, and isolation await children with ADHD. They often feel inadequate, bad or stupid because of not being able to meet the expectations of teachers and family. Teachers and parents might tell them that they are lazy for not doing better in school. They may act out some of their feelings by becoming aggressive, getting into fights, or striking out. This only alienates them more until they are identified as problems and then all areas of their lives are impacted. Identifying the problem is only the first step on the journey to wellness. The path taken is different depending on the medical advice given or available to them. Is ADHD a developmental disability, often hereditary, which is caused by delayed brain reaction? Minor brain damage has not been proven as yet to be a cause of ADD, but scientists are conducting research into this area. Could the symptoms be the result of another underlying cause? Could the brain be reacting negatively because it is reacting to allergens it is coming in contact with on a daily basis? Is ADD or ADHD brought on due to deficiency of essential vitamins (B complex), sugar, minerals, or other nutrients? Is it a genetic disorder? Or is it due to an after-effect of certain childhood procedures, like immunizations?

Read on to explore the answer yourself!

A CLOSER VIEW OF AN ADHD CHILD THROUGH THE YEARS

I was restless and hyperactive all my life. I couldn't keep up with my fast moving thoughts. My mind always ran 200 miles per hour ever since I can remember. My body trembled if I sat still. I felt as if something was crawling on me all the time. I constantly felt a tingling all over my body. I had to keep moving and twisting, even when I was sitting. When I stood up I rocked myself. I had a deep fear that something was going to explode inside me. I always feared that someone was out to get me; someone was going to tell on me and get me into trouble. I couldn't sleep well at night and had nightmares. I could not complete any work. My parents were alcoholics. Most of the time I couldn't talk to them or communicate in a normal way. I was sad and frustrated. I developed behavioral problems. My parents thought that I was lazy. They tried to discipline me many times.

In those days, if a child didn't feel good, people thought that it was due to laziness or lack of discipline. The well-known treatment for such problems in my house was "spanking" till the blood splattered. My parents, teachers and relatives didn't understand me. They all thought I was strange. I had an enormous amount of rage inside of me. My family doctor gave me a medication to calm me. I was to take the drug three times a day, but I often forgot. Whenever I forgot to take the medication, I always got into trouble. Every now and then I couldn't contain my rage. One day I got mad at my younger sister and beat her up. I also beat up one of the kids from the neighborhood. I felt very bad for being violent, like my father. Then one day an older neighborhood kid gave me a real drug to calm me down; for the first time in my life I took marijuana. It helped me to forget the pain. I never touched alcohol in my life. I was well built and didn't have any physical abnormalities, just a restless mind and body.

By the time I was a teenager, I had learned to mask my restlessness and internal trembling. I didn't have any close friends. The guy who supplied me with drugs became my only friend. I wouldn't really call him a friend. I was shy and afraid to talk to others. I was afraid to make friends because I thought, they might find out about my problem and consider me abnormal. I lived with my fears and pain, a prisoner inside myself. I completed school with great difficulty. Then I secured a job with General Motors, but was fired after a few months. I was hired and fired more often than you can imagine. Everybody including my family and neighbors thought I was a loser and that I couldn't even hold a job for a few months! I began hating my family and neighbors. I tried to avoid meeting them by staying away from my home and neighborhood during the day, and returning home late at night. I wandered here and there to kill many boring hours.

I moved away from my little hometown as soon as I had the first chance and went to Los Angeles to visit a distant aunt. I decided to stay there and try to find a job, hoping to make a new life in the new city among strangers who knew nothing about my past. Somehow I struggled along.

I had several jobs in LA, but I couldn't stay in any of them. For a while, I felt a little better in the new city. First of all, no one knew me. And no one had time to mind other people's business in the busy city. My heart yearned to be like other normal people. But I didn't know how. I compared myself to others. There was something about me that was not normal. I read a lot and searched silently for answers to my problems. I joined meditation and yoga groups along with exercise classes. I changed my diet, ate organic foods, and took lots of vitamins. I practiced relaxation techniques every day, very faithfully. When I was 35, I started to experience anxiety attacks. I felt awful most of the time. I often felt as if I was having a heart attack, with pain starting in my chest (my father and grandfather have had heart attacks). It caused me to worry and I would start to hyperventilate. I was tired most of the time and I felt as if I was dragging myself through life. Before long, I worked myself into a complete ball of terror that couldn't be controlled. I started going to the emergency room at a local well-known hospital. The nurses would take my blood pressure and the doctors would give me a pill to calm me down. They said I was fine; it's just a case of nerves!

By the third visit they sent me to the staff psychiatrist. He ran blood tests, X-Rays etc., and concluded that I was just a nervous person. He prescribed a pill called Tofranil to take 4 times a day. I took it for a week, but still had panic attacks, so I called the doctor back. He increased the dosage to 10 pills per day. I wasn't comfortable with that, so I moved on. A friend suggested that I go to a psychiatrist who specialized in panic disorders. He interviewed me for 30 minutes and concluded that a chemical imbalance caused my anxiety. He had me take a blood test and gave me a book to read about manic depression. Oh, and he also gave me all the Zanax (antidepressant Valium) I needed. I averaged 5 to 7 pills per day. On my next visit, he told me that I should take a pill called Paxil (antidepressant) daily. I asked how long I had to take it and he indicated that he didn't know, perhaps forever.

I had sunk as low as I could. My brain was imbalanced and after months of attacks I was fired from my job (they later told people I was a drug addict and couldn't keep it together). I couldn't hold a job and wasn't strong enough to go through the red tape to receive state aid. My financial situation was grave to say the least. I took Paxil and Zanax for months and didn't have as many attacks; however, I was *so subdued from chemicals that I didn't really exist. I became addicted to Zanax (those people at last were proven right). Then I looked for other answers. I went to therapy and talked about how my dad spanked me when I was ten because of this and that. Still I felt terrible. Then I found a doctor who had a new drug, Busbar. I bought 100 of them at a dollar a piece. I took one pill and staggered around the house for hours, as if I had a pint of whiskey! I called the doctor the next day and asked him if he'd ever taken Busbar before. He meekly said, "no." As I slammed the phone down in disgust, I decided I wasn't taking any more pills and threw the other 99 in the trash. I tried to put my life back together as best as I could.*

*A year and a half went by and I had no clue if I would ever be my "old self" again. I was working for a textile distributor and felt horrible all the time, aching and tired. I started having serious allergy symptoms: itchy eyes, sneezing and a runny nose. I'd always had allergies to weeds and pollen, but nothing this severe. I ate some shrimp and my eyes swelled shut. I went to a doctor and he told me to take antihistamines (great, more pills) and **not to eat shrimp ever again.***

Then one day, my roommate met someone who used to have allergies but went to an acupuncturist and felt much better. When he suggested that I go to this doctor, I said "why not; I had nothing to lose."

September 24, 1992 was my first visit to Dr. Nambudripad. I was given tests to find out what I was allergic to. I rated 90 to 100 to most of the items on the list. I was allergic to almost everything. Dr. Nambudripad talked to me for a few minutes and determined I was having an acute reaction to cotton. Every piece of clothing I was wearing was cotton and I spent 8 hours a day next to a 30-year-old ware-

house of cotton. She treated me for cotton and I started to feel better. I read "Say Good-bye to Illness," and learned that I probably inherited my allergy from my father who had asthma as a child. She also thought that I was reacting to the pesticides that were sprayed regularly in my hometown that caused all my fears, body aches, joint pains, and phobias. I was successfully treated for DDT and other pesticides. I grew up in a tiny village among farmers who sprayed DDT almost every week to kill mosquitoes and other bugs. I also learned that the pains in my chest were caused by gas in my stomach, which was produced by various food allergies, not heart attacks. I was relieved and I calmed down.

I had a series of treatments for two years; the most difficult one to pass was shellfish and vitamin A. I was very allergic to shellfish all my life. If I ate any trace of fish I would swell up like a balloon. I couldn't breathe. I ended up in the emergency room. Now, three years later, I can eat all the shrimp and lobster I want. After years of abstinence I can once again enjoy Chinese food.

I must admit at first I was apprehensive, but the fear passed because each time I ate shellfish there was no reaction. My energy and confidence returned. I now work at a leading IBM computer firm and earn a six figure salary. Yes, life is once again worth living. I've learned to test my allergies through a series of patient education classes that I attended at Dr. Devi's office. Now I know what to eat and what to buy (type of clothes and other items). I also know how to treat myself if I encounter an unexpected allergic reaction. "You have to take charge of your life," Dr. Nambudripad said to us at the patient education seminar. "No one knows your body better than you do. No one can understand your limitations," she said. I know it sounds unbelievable. But Dr. Nambudripad's allergy treatment techniques saved my life. She let me out of my jail. I have a life now, a life anyone would dream of. I am not afraid to talk to anyone any more. I don't have to hide my fears inside me any more. I have become such a believer in allergies and how they affect our bodies to a point where one can get completely destroyed. Now, I refer anyone I meet with allergies to Dr. Devi. Perhaps, one more life could be saved!

A few of my friends were able to overcome their skepticism and went to see Dr. Devi; all were pleased with the results. I have also met hundreds of other patients with horror stories of bouncing around the medical system without a proper diagnosis, treatment or a destination who finally turned their health around with NAET treatments. I pray that the millions who suffer now from allergy have access to Dr. Nambudripad's NAET treatments.

Thankfully,
Dennis Wilber
Huntington Beach/ CALIF.

This is the story of a real person who, like so many others around us, suffers from the frustrating and agonizing symptoms of attention deficit hyperactive disorder. For them normal living is difficult. During the course of maturing some children outgrow the typical hyperactive symptoms and lead a normal adulthood while others may develop different health disorders, or get progressively worse with their symptoms, making not only their lives, but also their families' lives miserable. In most cases of children who have been diagnosed as having ADD or ADHD, a clear diagnosis is difficult because they do not exhibit the typical symptoms. Their symptoms often confuse and frustrate patients and their doctors, and place tremendous stress on their families and employers.

The heavy doses of antidepressants and stimulants produce temporary relief from the presenting symptoms in a majority of ADHD patients. However, the possibility of relapse awaits just around the corner. The side effects of these medications increase the risk of getting other health disorders or addictions in hypersensitive or allergic people.

Is there a Relationship between Allergy and ADHD?

In my NAET allergy practice, I have found working with ADHD children and their parents to be challenging. But, by treating with NAET, I have been able to receive a great amount of satisfaction and success in ADD and ADHD patients. I have treated over two hundred patients from different age groups who were diagnosed as suffering from attention deficit hyperactive disorders in the last three years. One group was clearly diagnosed as ADHD by appropriate medical practitioners and their diagnosis was supp-orted by various tests. The other group never had any concise diagnosis, yet suffered from the typical symptoms. In both groups, normal living was difficult until they were treated with NAET.

When I examined them using NTT (Nambudripad's Testing Techniques), regardless of the labels they carry, I found both groups suffered from various food and environmental allergies. When I treated them with NAET (Nambudripad's Allergy Elimination Techniques), both groups responded very well making it possible to eliminate their symptoms and live a normal life. In my practice, I have over 80% success in treating an ADD or ADHD patient regardless of his/her age.

It seems that many cases I see in my practice with ADHD have been misdiagnosed. Allergies affecting the brain and the nervous system can mimic ADHD easily. If the practitioner is not well informed about allergies and allergy-related symptoms, it is easy to misdiagnose ADHD since there is no definite laboratory tests that can identify an ADHD person.

Simple MRT can be used to detect the brain irritant easily. Once detected ADHD person should avoid the use or contact with the irritant This test can be mastered by any lay person. MRT is explained in detail in Chapter 6.

In this book, I am going to demonstrate how allergy to foods, environments, childhood immunizations, vaccinations, lacking certain internal body secretions, or producing abnormal enzymes, can generate, complicate or exaggerate the symptoms of ADD and ADHD. I will educate you about a simple testing procedure that will enable you to test your child in the privacy of your own home, and inform you about NAET, the procedure that can help to remove allergies and allergy related diseases. I will describe some techniques that can help to improve your child's attention span and reduce the hyperactivity of his/her brain, which will balance the body and mind during the journey through NAET.

An allergic reaction may be manifested in varying degrees as mild to severe irritability of the brain and nervous system, ADD, ADHD, itching, rashes, hives, edema, asthma, joint pains, muscle aches, headaches, restlessness, insomnia, addictions, cravings, indigestion, vomiting, anger, depression, irritability, hyperactivity, disturbed vision, poor attention span, panic attacks, brain fatigue, and brain fog.

When you look at an allergy from a holistic point of view, you can say that an allergy is an energy imbalance caused by the clashing of two or more incompatible charges. This is similar to like-magnetic charges repelling one another with a slight difference. The repulsion of the incompatible energies causes an allergic reaction, an altered action in the body.

The symptoms, diagnosis and treatment of sensitivities, hypersensitivities and intolerances, (non-IgE mediated reactions), and allergies (IgE mediated reactions) often overlap. Both intolerances and allergies, in varying degrees, can be tested by Muscle Response Testing (MRT) either by producing a weak MRT (weakness of the indicator muscle in the case of an allergy), or a strong MRT (strong resistance by the indicator muscle in the case of no allergy). All of these allergic reactions are capable of producing ADHD, but can successfully be treated by NAET. MRT and NAET are explained in detail in Chapter Six.

SHOULD DRUGS BE USED TO CONTROL ADHD SYMPTOMS?

There is a big controversy in the use of stimulants in people with ADHD. Ever since the appearance of Ritalin and other stimulants many children have been helped to perform better in school, to behave more appropriately in social circles, and to cooperate at home with their families. These children, who benefitted from the use of stimulants, probably did not have allergies to the drugs. Just like any other allergy -- children did not have an allergy to Ritalin, and it worked like a magic bullet for them. These children were able to control their symptoms and go through the learning process as other average children and once matured, 50% of the children were able to outgrow the symptoms and lead a normal life.

At the same time a large percentage of children were allergic to the drugs, and did not respond to them. Instead they suffered from numerous side effects that practically ruined their lives. Parents of such children unanimously blamed the drugs as a bad treatment choice for ADHD children. No one thought about the allergy interfering with the treatment result. Some practitioners, without taking allergy into consideration, continued to prescribe the magic bullets for the children. When the children looked like zombies or turned into robots, when their brain almost shut down, or in some cases when they became uncontrollably violent, when they ended up having many other health problems, the family and the practitioners were equally disappointed. Is it any wonder that this misconception about using stimulants or antidepressants instilled fear in families of ADHD children, and the media?

On the contrary, children who do not receive help in controlling their ADHD symptoms by some means or therapy may grow up as frustrated, angry adults or end up as school dropouts, social outcasts or even criminals.

We cannot ignore the scientific achievements of the drug industry. Sometimes drugs are useful or necessary to control the acute symptoms. There is nothing wrong in using drugs to reduce or control the severe symptoms where it is needed. However, there are rules for the successful usage of drugs:

♦ First, and most importantly, the practitioner should check the drug for any possible allergy.

♦ It should be used wisely and only when it is absolutely necessary.

♦ It should be used only to achieve a short term goal.

♦ The cause of the problems should be identified and eliminated as soon as possible.

♦ The drug should be replaced with a natural effective substitute (therapy, herbs etc.) soon after the acute problem is solved.

Sometimes, drug usage is necessary even in the treatments with NAET. I encourage the use of drugs in the initial stages of NAET treatments. If the presenting symptoms are kept under control, NAET treatments will work better. But one problem I often encounter is that most people are reactive and highly allergic to the very drug that is supposed to help them stabilize their brain.

People suffer from many side effects of drugs, ranging from mild skin rashes to severe hives all over the body, indigestion to severe vomiting and diarrhea, tiredness to extreme fatigue, shortness of breath to severe asthma, and fainting to anaphylaxis. So before administering any drug, the practitioner should test the patient carefully for a possible allergy to the drug before prescribing it. If found, it should be treated immediately. An allergy to drugs can harm the patient more than any other toxin you can think of. Allergy and its side effects can easily be removed with NAET without going through extensive and expensive invasive procedures; and the patient will be able to use it as needed to keep his/her symptoms under control before treating or looking for other causes.

An allergy is a hereditary condition: an allergic predisposition or tendency is inherited, but the allergy itself may not manifest until some later date. Researchers have found that when both parents were or are allergy-sensitive, 75 to 100 percent of their offspring react to those same allergens. When neither of the parents is (nor was) sensitive to allergens, the probability of producing allergic offspring drops dramatically to less than 10 percent. Most of us suffer from allergic manifestation in varying degrees because of our different levels of parental inheritance.

Studies have shown that, in some cases, even when parents had no allergies, their offspring still suffered from many allergies since birth. In these cases, various possibilities exist:

♦ Parents may have suffered from a serious disease or condition. For example, the parents had rheumatic fever before the child was born, which caused an alteration in the genetic codes.

♦ The pregnant mother may have been exposed to harmful substances such as radiation (X-rays); chemicals (an expectant mother taking too much caffeine, alcohol, drugs or antibiotics, chemical exposures, carbon monoxide poisoning, etc.); circulating internal toxins as the result of a disease (streptococcal infection as in strep throat, measles, chicken pox, candidiasis, parasitic infestation, diabetes, etc.); emotional trauma (sudden loss of loved ones, various kinds of abuses like mental torture, rapes, fearful falls, financial struggles, traumatic law suits, continuous harassment by others, etc.).

♦ The parents may have suffered severe malnutrition (not getting enough food or not assimililating due to poor absorption or allergies) possibly causing the growing embryo to undergo cell mutation during its development in the womb. The altered cells do not carry over the original genetic codes or do not go through normal development. The organs and tissues that are supposed to develop from the affected cells have impaired function.

♦ In our modern day life, many parents leave their infants in front of the color television permitting the infant to bathe in continuous flow of radiation for hours. Excess assimilation of television radiation can cause energy blockages and cell mutation in the growing infant.

We cannot ignore the fact that we are moving toward the twenty-first century where technology will be even more predominant than today. There is nothing wrong with the technology, but the allergic patient must find ways to overcome adverse reactions to chemicals and other allergens, in order to live a better life.

WHAT IS NAET?

A thorough treatise on biochemistry is not appropriate for the purpose of an introduction to this new method of treatment for people suffering from allergies. Instead, this discussion will concentrate on the basic constructs of this treatment method and give some insight into the lives of people that it has helped. This is not a new technology. It is actually a combination of knowledge and techniques that uses much of what is already known from allopathic (western medical knowledge), chiropractic, kinesiology, acupuncture (oriental medical knowledge) and nutrition. Each of the disciplines I studied provided bits of knowledge, which I used to develop this new allergy elimination treatment. There is no known successful method of treatment for food allergies using western medicine except avoidance, which means deprivation and frustration.

I developed this new technique of allergy and allergy-related symptom elimination, employing the knowledge from these above mentioned fields of medicine, to identify and treat the reactions to many substances, including food, chemicals, and environmental allergens.

Through many long years of research, and after many trials and errors, I devised this combination of "hands-on techniques" to eliminate energy blockages (allergies) permanently and to restore the body to a healthy state. These energy blockage elimination techniques together are called Nambudripad's Allergy Elimination Techniques or NAET for short.

ALLOPATHY AND WESTERN SCIENCE.

Knowledge of the brain, cranial nerves, spinal nerves and autonomic nervous system from western medicine enlightens us about the body's efficient multilevel communication network. Through this network of nerves, vital energy circulates in the body carrying negative and positive messages from each aṇd every cell to the brain and then back to the cells. A cell or tissue sends one message to brain. The brain sends out the reply in a matter of nano-seconds to the rest of the body. Knowledge about the nervous system, its origin, travel route, organs and tissues that benefit from its nerve energy supply (target organs and tissues), helps us to understand the energy distribution of the spinal nerves emerging from the 31 pairs of spinal nerve roots. If the energy supply reaches all the respective organs and tissues, through their miles-long nerve fibers, they all remain healthy and happy. If the energy distribution is reduced or stopped in one or more of the spinal nerves, the respective organs and tissues will have diminished function or partial or complete shut down. By evaluating the condition of its target organs and tissues, changes in energy distribution via any spinal nerve can be detected (Gray's Anatomy-36th edition).

KINESIOLOGY

Kinesiology is the art and science of movement of the human body. Kinesiology is used in NAET to compare the strength and weakness of any muscle of the body in the presence or absence of any substance. This is also called Muscle Response Testing to detect allergies. It is hypothesized that this measurable weakness of a particular muscle is produced by the generation of an energy obstruction in the particular spinal nerve route that corresponds to the weakened muscle when the specific item is in its energy field. Any item that is capable of producing energy obstruction in any spinal nerve route is called an allergen. Through this simple kinesiological testing method allergens can be detected; obstructed spinal nerves and their routes can be identified; and the affected organs, tissues, and other body parts can be uncovered.

CHIROPRACTIC

Chiropractic technique helps us to detect the nerve energy blockage in a specific nerve energy pathway by detecting and isolating the exact nerve root that is being pinched. The exact vertebral level in relation to the pinched spinal nerve root helps us to trace the travel route, the destination and the target organs of that particular energy pathway. D.D.Palmer, who is considered the "Father of Chiropractic" said, "too much or too little energy is disease." According to chiropractic theory, a pinched nerve can cause disturbance in the energy flow. Earlier we saw that the presence of an allergen in its energy field can cause a pinched nerve or obstruction of the nerve energy flow. Chiropractic medicine postulates that a pinched nerve or any such disturbance in the energy flow can cause disease in the target organ and tissues, revealing the importance of maintaining an uninterrupted flow of nerve energy. A pinched nerve or an obstruction in the energy flow can result from an allergy. Spinal manipulation at the specific vertebral level of the pinched nerve can relieve the obstruction of the energy flow and help the body come to a state of homeostasis (i.e. a state of perfect balance between all energies and functions).

ACUPUNCTURE/ ORIENTAL MEDICINE

Yin-Yang theory from oriental medical principles also teaches the importance of maintaining homeostasis in the body. According to oriental medical principles, "when the Yin and Yang are balanced in the body, (a state of perfect balance between all energies and functions), no disease is possible." Any disturbance in the homeostasis can cause disease. Any allergen that is capable of producing a weakening effect of the muscles in the body can cause disturbance in the homeostasis. By isolating and eliminating the cause of the disturbance (in this case an allergen), and by maintaining an absolute homeostasis, diseases can be prevented and cured. According to acupuncture theory, acupuncture and/or acupressure at certain acupuncture points are capable of bringing the body into a state of homeostasis, by removing the energy blockages from the twelve (meridian) energy pathways.When the blockages are removed, energy can flow freely through the energy meridians bringing the body into perfect balance.

NUTRITION

You are what you eat! The secret to good health is achieved through correct nutrition. What is correct nutrition? How do you get it? When you can eat nutritious food without discomfort and assimilate the nutrients from the food, that food is said to be the right food. When you get indigestion, bloating, and other digestive troubles upon or after eating a particular food, that food is not helping you to function normally. However natural, expensive or packed with high quality nutrition, if a food item causes one or more of these symptoms upon ingestion, it is not the right nutrition for you. This is due to an allergy to that food. Different people react differently to the same food. So, it is very important to clear the allergy to the nutrients,which are in the food. Allergic people can tolerate food that is low in nutrition better than nutritious food. After clearing the allergy, you should try to eat more wholesome, nutritious foods. Above all, you should avoid refined, bleached food devoid of nurients.

Many people who feel poorly due to undiagnosed food allergies may take vitamins or other supplements to increase their vitality. This can actually make them feel worse if they happen to be allergic to these nutrients as well. Only after clearing those allergies can their bodies properly assimilate them. So nutritional assessment should be done periodically, and if needed, appropriate supplements should be taken to receive better results.

We need the complete cooperation of the whole brain and nervous system to get the best results with NAET. NAET involves the whole brain and its network of nerves, as it reprograms the brain by erasing previously harmful memory regarding the allergen and imprints the new useful memory in its place.

INCOMPATIBILITIES / IMBALANCES

The energy blockages in the human body are caused by incompatible electro-magnetic charges around the body. When there is an incompatible charge around the body, there is an altered reaction in the body. Energy incompatibilities that are capable of producing various ailments are used synonymously with "allergy" in this book.

When we talk about health conditions, there is hardly a human disease or condition that may not involve an allergic factor; attention-deficit hyperactive disorder is not any different. Any portion of the body, organ, or group of organs may be involved, though the allergic responses may vary greatly from one item to another and from one person to another.

In 1983, I originated NAET to eliminate allergic reactions and successfully restore normal functions of the body by manipulating the spinal nerves. Major illnesses, severe reactions to drugs, toxins, chemicals, radiation, emotional stresses, etc., are capable of causing damage to the sensory nerve fibers and inhibiting their conductivity. Allergy and allergy-related illnesses can thus be eliminated or reduced in their intensity by treating with NAET.

The brain, through 31 pairs of spinal nerves, operates the best network of communication ever known. Energy blockages take place in a person's body due to contact with adverse energy of other substances. When two adverse energies come close, repulsion takes place. When two compatible energies get together, attraction takes place.

NAET can unblock the blockages in the energy pathways and restart normal energy circulation through the energy channels. This will, in turn, help the brain to work and coordinate with the rest of the body to operate the body functions appropriately. When the brain is not coordinating with the vital organs, physiological functions are impaired.

When the energy circulation in the energy pathways is restored, the vital organs resume their routine work and function properly.The brain and body together will remove any toxic build-up through the body's natural excretory mechanisms.

When the energy channels are filled with vibrant energy, and the energy circulates through the channels freely, the body is said to be in perfect balance or in homeostasis. When the body is in homeostasis, it can function normally, and allergies and diseases do not affect the body. In this state, the body can absorb all the necessary nutrients from the foods consumed.

The energy channels need energy to function normally. This energy is produced from the nutrients consumed, such as vitamins, minerals, and sugars, etc. The attraction or repulsion of the electromagnetic energy field is created in the body by the interaction of the various charged nutrients inside the body. Each cell is an electricity-generating unit loaded with positively charged potassium and some sodium. Most of the sodium is outside the cell. The sodium and potassium keep circulating in and out of the cell in the presence of water with the help of other nutrients like proteins and sugars. These charged molecules inside the body make the whole body an electrical unit with an electrical field around it.

When the sympathetic and parasympathetic nerves are not coordinating well, the highly blocked area or the weakest parts of the body fails first. If the energy supply to the brain is blocked abnormalities in the function of the brain is seen: A person can demonstrate attention-deficit hyperactive disorders, manic depressive disorders, schizophrenic, and other neurological disorders, etc.

These nearly 90% effective, successful NAET treatments are available to the whole world. It is up to the health professionals to learn them and use them on their patients, and it is up to the public to get them from their doctors to receive full benefits of this new, remarkably effective treatment method.

Thousands of doctors of allopathic, chiropractic, osteopathy, dentistry, naturopathy, and acupuncture/oriental medicine from all over the United States, Canada, Europe, Australia, Asia and other countries, have been trained to treat their patients with this new revolutionary technique. Regular training sessions are being conducted several times a year to prepare many more licensed medical professionals to meet the challenge. This book will educate individuals to test themselves and locate the cause of their problem. Steps of treatments are not given here, because that is beyond the scope of this book. The information about the NAET training available for licensed medical practitioners can be received from the following sources:

NAET
6714 Beach Blvd,
Buena Park, CA 90621
Tel: I-714-523-0800 / (714) 523 8900
Fax: 1-714-523-3068
E-mail: naet@earthlink.net
Web site: naet.com

CHAPTER TWO

ADHD? OR BRAIN ALLERGY?

2

ADHD OR BRAIN ALLERGY?

Statistics indicate that approximately 3–5% of school age children in the United States have been diagnosed as suffering from some form of allergy and allergy related diseases. My experience has shown that most of the cases of ADD and ADHD are the result of undiagnosed allergies.

The shocking fact is that there are hardly any human diseases or conditions in which allergic factors are not involved directly or indirectly. Any substance under the sun, including sunlight itself, can cause an allergic reaction in any individual. In other words, potentially, you can be allergic to anything you come in contact with. If you begin to check people around you—not only people with ADHD, even so called healthy people—you will find them reacting to many things around them.

You can be allergic to: foods, drinks, drugs, childhood immunizations, herbs, vitamins, water, clothing, jewelry, cold, heat, wind, food colors, additives, preservatives, chemicals, formaldehyde, etc. Undiagnosed allergies can produce symptoms of various health disorders including ADD and ADHD at any age.

By learning the simple Nambudripad's Testing Technique (NTT), anyone, professional or layman, can easily learn to recognize various allergens and the health conditions they cause. This will help the sufferer begin to seek the appropriate diagnostic studies and pursue proper health care as needed. When the patient's diagnosis is correct, results are less frightening than an uncertain diagnosis from a doctor.

Science and technology have altered the lifestyle of mankind enormously. The reactions and diseases arising from responses to these changes are also very different. Our quality of life has improved from these scientific achievements. Yet, these same scientific accomplishments have become everlasting nightmares for people suffering from attention deficit disorders.

Technology is becoming more pervasive over time. Let's face it, technology will always be with us. But ADD patients must find ways to overcome adverse reactions to new chemicals and other allergens created by the new technology they are exposed to. NAET will fit right in with the 21st century life style of the modern world. Even though it requires a series of detailed treatments, NTT and Nambudripad's Allergy Elimination treatments (NAET) offer the prospect of relief to people who suffer from constant irritations from allergies.

COMMONLY SEEN SYMPTOMS OF BRAIN DISORDERS

ALLERGY IN AN ADHD CHILD OR ADULT?

♦   Constant motion: climbing, jumping, bouncing back and forth, fidgeting, squirming, running, wiggling, swinging legs, and tapping utensils on the table.

♦   Biting: nails, fingers or chewing part of their clothes or biting other children.

- Restlessness: difficulty sitting quietly, tossing and turning in bed, unable to watch T.V. for few moments, or play a game.

- Incessant talking, thinking, speaking or babbling constantly, very involved in their own world and comforts, and inconsiderate of others, etc.

- Focusing: doesn't pay attention to what is being said or doesn't pay attention to details, easily distracted by others or other stimuli, day dreams, and procrastinations.

- Organizational skills: difficulty organizing tasks, often loses things necessary for completing tasks, forgets daily events, leaves a mess around them.

- Responsibility: not being on time, not taking responsibility for their own actions and/or blaming someone else for his / her actions.

- Self-Control: Blurts out answers to questions before being asked, unable to wait in line, or wait their turn, acts before thinking.

- Emotional: Easily angered, severe mood swings, aggressive, violent and hostile or extremely silly, clowning around, and socially embarrassing their loved ones.

- Stability: Changing jobs, friends, spouses, and relation ships often.

- Addictions: Easily addicted to alcohol, tobacco, caffeine, food (eating disorders), drugs, gambling, spending large amount of money without looking at the bank book; most criminals can fall in this group.

- Children and adults with ADHD also suffer from other health disorders and chronic diseases: burning eyes, runny nose, and restricted breathing, asthma, emphysema, chronic lung disorders, eye disorders, ear infections, upper respiratory complications, sinus troubles, chronic infections, inflammatory conditions, fibromyalgia, migraines, head aches, and various types of arthritis.

♦ Candida, yeast problems, parasite infestation, chronic fa tigue, immune disorders, hormonal imbalances, and pediatric problems.

♦ Autism, many mental disorders, anxiety, depression, and various emotional imbalances, etc.

♦ Circulatory disorders, sleep irregularity, chemical sensitivity, nutritional disorders, restless leg syndrome, skin ailments, and genito-urinary disorders.

This clearly points out that there are no typical responses to allergens in the real world. If we are depending on allergies to produce a uniform set of responses for all people, we may misdiagnose and provide the wrong treatment. We cannot duplicate and package a standard medication as an antidote for any specific allergy—each individual case is different. We must not oversimplify our treatment of patients. Not everyone exhibits typical allergic symptoms (whatever we perceive typical to be). Should we do so, we risk missing a myriad of potential reactions that may be produced in some people in response to their contact with substances - that are for them - allergens.

CATEGORIES OF ALLERGENS

Common allergens are generally classified into nine basic categories; based primarily on the method in which they are contacted, rather than the symptoms they produce.

1. Inhalants
2. Ingestants
3. Contactants
4. Injectants
5. Infectants
6. Physical Agents
7. Genetic Factors
8. Molds and Fungi
9. Emotional Factors

INHALANTS

Inhalants are those allergens that are contacted through the nose, throat and bronchial tubes. Examples of inhalants are microscopic spores of certain grasses, flowers, pollens, powders, smoke, cosmetics, perfumes, different aromas from spices, coffee, popcorn, food-cooking smells, different herbs and oils and chemical fumes such as paint, varnish, pesticides, insecticides, fertilizers, and flour from grains, etc.

It is typical for a person with ADD to react to most of these environmental allergens. The symptoms of an ADD person arising from the interactions with the above allergens, varies greatly from a typical response of an environmentally sensitive person. In an ADHD person the first organ in the body that is affected is the brain and the typical symptoms of brain allergy are exhibited.

I WAS DIAGNOSED WITH ADHD

As a child, I was plagued with Attention Deficit Disorder and was given lots of drugs. I suffered from allergies to dust and pollens, severe restlessness, violent nightmares, numbness in my hands, and various fears and phobias. I am now a 46-year-old male with a lifelong history of mental illness.

My mother had to spend many hours coaching me with schoolwork. With her help, I did well in school. When I was 18-years-old, I had a breakdown during college freshman orientation week. I became very depressed and started psychiatric treatment. I was seen by numerous psychiatrists and hospitalized in as many places.

Over the years both conventional psychiatrists as well as doctors who practice alternative medicine treated me. As each new drug or vitamin therapy came along I tried it with much hope and anticipation. However, none of them produced the results I had hoped for: stable moods.

With age, my condition had deteriorated to the point where my family was afraid they would have to institutionalize me.

It was at this point that I began to see Dr. Devi Nambudripad. During my first few months of treatment, I noticed that no matter which end of the waiting area I sat in, everyone else was choosing seats at the other end. Because of the severity of my condition, the treatments had to proceed slowly.

I had an especially difficult time with chemicals in artificial colors, flavors, sweeteners, preservatives, pesticides, and cleaners, etc. After a few months of treatment, I started to have an occasional good day; one judged to be emotionally stable. When I went to her office, people began choosing their seats closer to me and began conversations.

As time went on, I worked my way through the treatment list, my good days started to outnumber the bad.

After 2 years of treatment, I rarely have a bad day and never one that's so bad that I cannot control my emotions in public. I am now on a minimum dose of medication and hope to eliminate all drugs. I come from a family of health professionals who are very supportive. My family is involved in my NAET treatments. I feel that, considering the seriousness of my mental condition, my family's involvement was critical to my success. I would like to say after living with mental illness my entire life, it's great to see the light at the end of that dark tunnel.

John Mitchel
Fullerton, CA

INGESTANTS

Ingestants are allergens, which are contacted through the mouth and find their way into the gastrointestinal tract. These include foods, condiments, drugs, beverages, chewing gum, and vitamin supplements, etc. We must not ignore the potential reactions to things that are touched, then inadvertently transmitted into the mouth through our hands.

The area of ingested allergens is one of the most difficult to diagnose because the allergic responses are often delayed from several minutes to several days. This makes the direct association between cause and effect very difficult. Some people can react violently in seconds after they consume an allergen. In extreme cases, just touching or coming near the allergen is enough to forewarn the central nervous system that it is about to be poisoned resulting in a premature allergic reaction. Usually more violent reactions are observed in ingested allergens than in any other forms.

Such was the case of eight-year-old Don, who complained of having a stomach ache every day for six months. He became very irritable at times. His parents noticed how his personality was changing. He was becoming antisocial, refusing to go out and play with other children. He stayed home when he was not in school. He did not do his schoolwork or homework and began to get poor grades. His teacher reported that he was turning into a loner. His parents were called to the school many times because of his problems. They took Don to the pediatrician, after administering a battery of tests, he was diagnosed as having ADHD.

One of his mother's friends, whose son was successfully treated by me for celiac disease, had similar symptoms and behavioral problems initially. He became normal when the celiac disease was under control by treating with NAET. She referred him to us. Don was examined by NTT, and found to be allergic to 18 basic groups of foods from the NAET list. His treatments were very successful until he reached the grain mix. He failed grain mix three times. He was highly allergic to the wheat and gluten in the mix, which caused him to fail the treatment. His strange behavior and stomach ache was under control when he passed the treatment for grain mix.

We live in a highly technological age. New substances are being introduced into our diets to preserve color, flavor, and extend the shelf life of our foods. There are some additives used in foods as preservatives that have caused severe health problems. Some artificial sweeteners cause mysterious problems in particular people. They may mimic symptoms of serious disorders (ADD, hyperactivity, frontal lobe irritation, autism, bipolar disorder, anxiety disorder, obsessive compulsive disorder, personality problems, and manic depressive disorder, etc.). Clinical depression, anti-social behaviors, itching and hives, insomnia, vertigo, are also reactions from an allergy to food coloring and preservatives. The majority of these additives are harmless to most people but can be disabling and life-threatening to those who react to these substances.

Great care must be taken to know exactly what is contained in anything a person with allergies puts into his mouth. If everyone could become proficient in MRT, simple testing before eating foods could prevent most hazardous reactions from food allergies.

CONTACTANTS

Contactants produce their effect by direct contact with the skin. They include environmental allergens, fabrics, cats, dogs, rabbits, cosmetics, soaps, skin creams, detergents, rubbing alcohol, latex gloves, hair dyes, various types of plant oils, and chemicals such as gasoline, dyes, acrylic nails, nail polish, fabrics, formaldehyde, etc.

Allergic reactions to contactants can be different in each person, and may produce hyperactivity, distractibility and impulsivity in people with ADHD

Various natural or synthetic fabrics can cause brain irritability in ADD persons. Many people react to cotton. Cotton is used in numerous items. It is not easy to find a fabric that is made from only one type of material anymore. Many products seen in shops are a blend of many things. Cotton fibers are used in carpets, elastics, bed sheet, fleece material, cosmetic applicators, toilete paper, paper towels, etc. Wool may also cause brain imbalances in sensitive persons. Some people who are sensitive to wool also react to creams with a lanolin base since lanolin is derived from sheep wool. Some people can be allergic to cotton socks, nylon socks or woolen socks, causing them to have abnormal and irrational behaviors. People can also be allergic to carpets and drapes that can cause similar reactions in sensitive individuals.

Usually, female patients are allergic to their pantyhose and suffer from leg cramps, swollen legs, high blood pressure, headaches, mood swings and crying spells. Toilet paper and paper towels also cause problems mimicking similar reactions in many people.

A lot of people are allergic to crude oils, plant oils and their derivatives, which include plastic and synthetic rubber products as well as latex products. Can you imagine the difficulty of living in this modern society, attempting to be completely free from products made of crude oil? A person would literally be immobilized. The phones we use, the milk containers we drink from, the polyester fabrics we wear, most of the face and body creams we use... all are made from a common product – crude oil!

Food items normally classified as ingestants—may also act as contactants on persons who handle them constantly over time. They can cause migraines, headaches, brain irritability, anger, and depression, etc.

Other career-produced allergies have been diagnosed in cooks, waiters, grocery store-keepers, clerks, gardeners, etc. Virtually no trade or skill is exempt from contacting allergens and producing allergic symptoms.

A writer by profession, Nelly was completely disabled with her nervous stomach, irritable bowel syndrome, insomnia, and heart palpitations. She was easily angered and had sinusitis and postnasal drip for seven years. She was given an NTT evaluation and it was found that she was allergic to newspaper ink and all kinds of paper including toilet paper, and dollar bills. Nelly was simply allergic to the paper she wrote on. Her symptoms started seven years ago, not long after she began her career as a writer. After she was treated for all the NAET basics and the paper products by NAET, her symptoms cleared.

Another case of a paper allergy was observed during an interview with an attorney who complained that he always came away from his office with a severe headache. His personality would change and he would become hostile and angery at the least little thing. His family would hide in another room not to be in his way. The attorney was allergic to paper—but his reaction was completely different from that of the professional writer.

INJECTANTS

Allergens are injected into the skin, muscles, joints and blood vessels in the form of various serums, antitoxins, vaccines, childhood immunizations, and drugs. Injectants also include substances entering the body through insect bites. As with any other allergic reaction, the injection of a sensitive drug into the system creates the risk of producing dangerous allergic reactions. To the sensitive person, the drug actively becomes a poison with the same effect as an injection of arsenic. The seemingly harmless substance can become more allergenic for certain people over time without the person being aware of the potential risk. For example, take the increasing number of incidents of allergies to the drug penicillin. The reactions vary from hives to diarrhea to anaphylactic shock and death.

Various vaccinations and immunizations may also produce such allergic reactions. After receiving their usual immunizations, some children become extremely ill physically, physiologically, and emotionally. Various neurological disorders, hyperactive disorders, attention deficit disorders, autism, mental retardation, manic disorders, Crohn's disease, chronic irritable bowel syndrome, tumors, and cysts, etc., could manifest as a delayed reaction of a childhood immunization.

Such was the case of a 6-year-old boy Danny, who became very sick after a regular DPT immunization. He had a continuous fever (102 degrees Fahrenheit) that lasted for six weeks. Finally, when the fever came down to a normal level, he became irritable, aggressive, short tempered, anti-social. He couldn't play with other children without kicking, hitting, biting or spitting on them. He talked constantly and craved sweets all the time. He ran around the house playing hide and seek in the middle of the night instead of sleeping. His worried parents brought him to see me. His problem was traced to the DPT immunization by testing using NTT. He was treated for all the basics and DPT vaccine with NAET. He became well again after he was treated for DPT.

INFECTANTS

Infectants are allergens that produce their effect by causing sensitivity to an infectious agent, such as bacteria. For example, an allergic reaction may result when tuberculin bacterium is introduced as part of a diagnostic test to determine a patient's sensitivity or reaction to it. A typical reaction to the tuberculin test may be seen as an infectious eruption under the skin. This type of reaction may occur with a skin patch or scratch tests preformed in the normal course of allergy testing in traditional medical approach.

Infectants differ from injectants because of the nature of the allergic substance; that is a substance, which is a known injectant and is limited in the amount administered to the patient. A slight prick of the skin introduces the toxin through the epidermis and a pox, or similar harmless skin lesion will erupt if the patient is allergic to that substance. For most people, the pox soon dries up and forms a scab that eventually heals, without much discomfort. However, in some cases the site of the injectant becomes infected and the usual inflammatory process can be seen (redness, swelling, pain, drainage of pus from the site for many days). Some sensitive individuals may experience fainting, nausea, fever, swelling (not only at the scratch site but also over the whole body), and respiratory distress, etc., if left untreated.

In other words, the introduction of an allergen into a reactive person's system creates the potential risk of causing a severe response regardless of the amount of the toxic substance used. Great care must be taken in the administration of traditional allergy testing procedures in highly sensitive individuals. However, if NAET is administered correctly and immediately it can stop such adverse reactions.

Teresa, a 31-year-old female born in one of the developing countries, was one of our unique cases. She manifested tremendous allergic reactions to a multitude of foods and objects in the environment. Her history revealed that when she was two-years-old, she suffered a severe reaction after a routine BCG vaccination. Her left hand swelled and she suffered from a high fever for weeks. She almost died from the infection. Medical help was not readily available in the part of the country where she grew up. Her parents migrated to the United States when she was seven-years-old. For many years she suffered physical allergies such as asthma, hives, joint pains, migraines, and gastrointestinal allergies (indigestion, heartburn, intermittent chronic diarrhea or constipation), and emotional reactions (depression, anger, crying spells, lacking interest in day-to-day activities, and severe pre-menstrual syndrome, etc.). When she was treated for all the basics, smallpox vaccination and bacteria mix by NAET, she was able to clear her allergic reactions to various items. Her physical, physiological, and emotional symptoms improved and stabilized swiftly after the treatment.

It should be noted that bacteria and virus are contacted in numerous ways. Our casual contact with objects and people exposes us daily to dangerous contaminants and possible illnesses. When our autoimmune systems are functioning properly, we pass off the illness without notice. It is when our systems are not working at maximum performance levels that we experience infections, fevers, and other discomforts.

From a strictly allergenic standpoint, however, contact with an injectant does not always produce the expected reaction. The intensity and type of reactions vary from individual to individual depending on their immune system, age and the amount of injectant received.

PHYSICAL AGENTS

Heat, humid air, cold, cold mist, sun radiation, dampness, drafts, changes in barometric pressure, high altitude, air conditioning; other types of radiation like computer, microwave, X-ray, geopathic radiation, electrical and electro-magnetic radiation, fluorescent lights, radiation from cellular and cordless telephones, and radiation from power lines are irritants. Vibrations from a washer and dryer, hair dryer, electric shaver, massager, motion vibrations from a moving automobile, motion sickness (car sickness, sea sickness), sickness while playing sports, roller coaster rides and/or horseback riding are mechanical irritants. Airplane sounds, traffic noises, loud music and voices in a particular pitch may also cause allergic reactions. All the above are known as physical allergens. Burns may also be included in this category. When the patient suffers from more than one allergy, physical agents can affect the patient greatly. If the patient has already eaten an allergic food item, then walks in cold air, he might develop upper respiratory problems, a sore throat, asthma or joint pains, etc., depending on his/her tendency toward particular health problems.

It is not uncommon for ADHD children to suffer from repeated canker sores. They suffer from sluggish digestion due to many food allergies, and food remains longer in the small bowel.

According to oriental medical principles, when food remains in the small bowel too long, the undigested food produces a large amount of heat. The heat escapes through the mouth causing the delicate mucous membrane of the mouth to blister and form canker sores. One of the young patients, Alan who came to our office had a history of canker sores whenever he ate pizza for dinner. He turned out to be highly allergic to tomato sauce (spices and tomato). After the basics, he was treated for tomato mix and pepper mix. He has never been bothered by canker sores again.

Many symptoms of ADD and ADHD patients become exaggerated on cold, cloudy or rainy days. The patients could suffer from a severe allergy to carbon dioxide (their own breath), electrolytes, cold or a combination of all. Some people, especially people who suffer from mental imbalances, also react to moonlight or moon radiation.

Some ADD or ADHD patients experience irritability, fear, and anxiety attacks when taking a hot shower. They are also allergic to humidity and can be successfully treated with NAET. A glass jar with a lid is filled half way with hot water. An NAET practitioner administers the NAET treatment while the patient holds the jar. In certain cases, salt is added to the hot water sample, creating salty and humid vapor (in order to treat someone who reacts to the atmosphere in coastal climates). Samples of very hot water used in treatment of mild to moderate types of burns have shown excellent results. Cold, high altitude, low altitude, wind, dampness, dryness, rainwater, and other physical agents can be treated in a similar way.

Some patients react to heat or cold violently, suffering from extreme chills and shaking uncontrollably. They need to bundle up with three-four layers of clothing during a cold day or experience icy cold hands and feet even if they are clad in mittens and warm socks. These patients are simply allergic to cold and combinations with other substances. An allergy to cold makes the blood sticky and the circulation will be poor. The body will not be able to get rid of its toxins. Allergy to anti-oxidants like vitamin C, A, etc. makes the elimination of the toxins difficult. If patients are allergic to iron, hormones, heat, etc., their reactions are just the opposite in hot weather. They feel very uneasy in the heat. They may need treatments for vitamin C, iron, cold, hormones, and their own blood, alone or in combination. When they finish the treatment program, they are less prone to feeling cold or getting sick with the changes in temperature.

GENETIC FACTORS

Discovery of possible tendencies toward allergies carried over from parents and grandparents open a large door to achieving optimum health. Most people inherit the allergic tendency from their parents or grandparents. Allergies can also skip generations or manifest differently in parents than in their children.

Bea, 38-years-old, had suffered from various allergies since she was an infant. When she was three-weeks-old, she broke out in a rash, which transformed into big heat boils. Her parents tried various medications in attempts to cure her; including allopathy, homeopathy, and herbal medicines. Finally, herbal medicine brought the problem somewhat under control. Even with the herbal treatment, she still occasionally suffered from outbreaks of skin lesions. When she was ten-years-old, she developed a type of severe, migraine headaches, severe insomnia, and mood swings, along with the arthritis.

After evaluation, she was found to be reacting to parasites. We learned that both her parents were in the Peace Corps before she was born. They were somehow infected with parasites and were seriously ill for months, but had no idea that their health problems were caused by the parasites until later. After she was treated successfully with NAET for parasites, her health took a quantum leap.

MOLDS AND FUNGI

Molds and fungi are in a category by themselves because of the numerous avenues through which they can come into contact with people in everyday life. They can be ingested, inhaled, touched, or even (as in the case of penicillin) injected. They can also come in the form of airborne spores making up a large part of the dust we breathe or pick up in our vacuum cleaners, in fluids such as our drinking water, the dark fungal growth in the corners of damp rooms. They can appear on the body as athlete's foot and in particularly fetid vaginal conditions commonly called "yeast infections." Molds and fungi also grow on trees and in the damp soil, are a source of food (truffles and mushrooms), disease (ringworm and the aforementioned yeast infections), and even of medicine (penicillin).

People with ADD and ADHD suffer from severe allergy to sugar, starches, and carbohydrates. Consumption and poor digestion of sugar products cause to create yeast, candida, etc. in the gut of the person. Overgrowth of these will cause them to travel to other parts of the body. Molds and fungi, belong to the same family and share the same energy fields. Reactions to these substances make people irritable, depressed, and suffer from a variety of mental imbalances, which can be easily mistaken for ADD and ADHD. When they get appropriate treatment to eliminate their yeast, candida, mold and fungi, they become symptom-free.

Allergies to feminine tampons, toilet papers, douches, and deodorants also cause yeast-like infections. One of the patients reacted to everything she ate from her freezer. More investigation proved that she was allergic to the fungus and molds found in the freezer.

My Granddaughter Was Allergic to Me!

Dear Dr. Devi,

My little granddaughter would not come near me. When I held out my arms to hold her, she would bury her head into the shoulder of whoever was holding her. If I had to take her to bathe or feed her, she would cry, get very cranky, aggressive, and irritable. At first I thought that she was tired, or teething. However, it happened constantly not to realize something was definitely amiss. I spoke to you and you immediately treated me for an allergy to my granddaughter. Two days later, when I saw my greatly loved grand baby— wonder of wonders—she ran into my arms! My first thought was thank you, Dr. Devi.

My grand daughter continues to rush into my arms, her face lights up when she sees me, she smiles, laughs, and now plays a little game with me, which previously she had not done.

It's a miracle! I maintain my attitude of deepest gratitude to Dr. Devi, her expertise and her NAET treatment program.

Kindest Regards,
Marilyn D. Nordquist, PhD.
Rancho Palos Verdes, CA

EMOTIONAL FACTORS

Various types of emotional allergies exists. We need to recognize them and eliminate them to be healthy. Until recently no one gave any importance to emotional blockages and the diseases arising from them. For years people with emotional problems were sent to psychiatrists, who labeled the suffers "mentally ill," and institutionized them. It was not recognized as a serious problem at the time. Emotional blockages can happen due to allergies, which affect the emotional aspect of the meridian or organ. If the blockages remain at the emotional level for a long period of time, they can begin to affect physical and physiological levels in the body, eventually turning into disease. Therefore, it is necessary to isolate and remove the cause of the emotional blockages as soon as possible. NAET deals with the whole body, removing blockages at the physical, physiological and emotional levels. Only then can a person be truly healthy. I have treated many hundreds of patients with emotional blockages. Children could be having a physical energy interference with his/her parents. This could cause irritation in the child's body and brain. Just like any other energy interference, this could cause ADD or ADHD symptoms in the victim. A few examples are given in Chapter 11. Parents should make a point to test the energy difference of the ADD or ADHD child between the mother, father, siblings, caretaker, baby sitter, friends, and their pets.

CHAPTER THREE

NAMBUDRIPAD'S TESTING
TECHNIQUES

3

NAMBUDRIPAD'S TESTING TECHNIQUES

S ymptoms of allergy vary from person to person depending upon the status of the immune system, degree of involvement of the organs and systems, age, and degree of inheritance. An allergy is a heredi- tary condition. An allergic predisposition is inherited, but may be manifested differently in family members.

There are many types of conventional allergy tests available to detect allergies; however, if it is done properly, the most reliable and convenient method of allergy testing is NTT testing. This is a modified form of kinesiological muscle testing. Allergies can be tested by NTT and treated very effectively with NAET. Please read Chapter 7 for more information on NTT and MRT.

NAMBUDRIPAD'S TESTING TECHNIQUES

1. History

A complete history of the patient is taken. A symptom survey form is given to the patient to record the level and type of discomfort he/she is suffering.

2. Physical examination

Observation of the mental status, face, skin, eyes, color, posture, movements, gait, tongue, scars, wounds, marks, body secretions, etc.

3. Vital signs

Evaluation of blood pressure, pulse, skin temperature and palpable energy blockages as pain or discomfort in the course of meridians, etc.

4. SRT

Skin Resistance Test for the presence or absence of a suspected allergen is done through a computerized electro-dermal testing device; differences in the meter reading are observed (greater the difference, stronger the allergy).

5. MRT

Muscle Response Testing is conducted to compare the strength of a pre-determined muscle in the presence and absence of a suspected allergen.

6. Dynamometer Testing

Hand-held dynamometer is used to measure finger strength (0-100) in the presence and absence of a suspected allergen. A hand-held dynamometer is used in this testing. The dynamometer is held with thumb and index finger and squeezed to make the reading needle swing between 0-100 scale. Initial baseline reading is observed first, then during contact with an allergen. The finger strength is compared in the presence of the allergen. If the second reading is more than the initial reading, there is no allergy. If the second reading is less than the initial reading, then there is an allergy. For example—if the initial (baseline) reading is 40 on a scale of 1-100, and if the reading in the presence of an allergen (apple) is 28—the person is allergic to the apple. If the second reading is 60- or 70- there is no allergy. Another benefit of dynamometer testing is that the degree of the weakness/strength is measured in numbers. This gives us some understanding of the degree of allergy.

7. MRT To Detect Allergies

Muscle Response Testing is the body's communication pathway to the brain. Through MRT, the patient can be tested for various allergens. MRT is a standard test used in applied kinesiology to compare the strength of a predetermined test muscle in the presence and absence of a suspected allergen. If the particular muscle (test muscle) weakens in the presence of an item, it signifies that the item is an allergen. If the muscle remains strong, the substance is not an allergen. More explanation on MRT will be given in Chapter 7.

8. SRT (Electro-Dermal Test-EDT)

After the MRT, the Skin Resistance Test (SRT) is administered. The patient is tested on a computerized instrument that is designed to painlessly measure the body's electrical conductivity at specific, electrically-sensitive points on the skin, particularly on the hands and feet.

The computerized tester also helps determine the various intensities of the allergies based on a 0 - 100 scale. This is probably one of the most accurate tests available today to determine allergies. The machine is designed to test food, environmental and chemical allergies, as well as allergies to molds, fungi, pollens, trees, grasses, proteins, vitamins, drugs, radiation, etc. It can be used to test allergies and their intensities before and after treatment so we are able to compare and show the body's response to the treatment.

The procedure does not involve breaking or puncturing the skin. There is no pain or discomfort. Hundreds of allergies can be tested on the patient in minutes. Since the testing probe only touches the skin for less than a second for each allergy tested, this method can be used for infants and children as well as adults. Another advantage of this machine is that it has a TV/computer monitor where the patient can read his/her own allergies as they are being recorded. A printout is produced and the data is saved for future comparison.

9. ALCAT Test

One of today's most reliable and effective tests to detect allergies and sensitivities to food, chemicals, and food additives is the ALCAT test. This system is designed to measure blood cell reactions to foods, chemicals, drugs, molds, pesticides, bacteria, etc. The methodology of this simple test includes using innovative laboratory reagents allowing accurate cell measurement in their native form. Individually processed test samples, when compared with the "Master Control" graph, will show cellular reactivity (cell count and size) if it has occurred. Scores are generated by relating these effective volumetric changes in white blood cells to the control curve.

10. Scratch Test

Although other available methods of allergy testing are plentiful, traditional methods of testing have never been very reliable. Western medical allergists generally depend on skin testing, (scratch test, patch test, etc.), in which a very small amount of a suspected allergic substance is introduced into the person's skin through a scratch or an injection. The site of injection is observed for any reaction. If there is any reaction at that area of injection, the person is considered to be allergic to that substance. Each item has to be tested individually.

This manner of testing is more dangerous, painful and time-consuming than SRT. Some patients can go into anaphylactic shock due to the introduction of extremely allergic items into the body. The painful procedure can cause soreness for several days. The patient must wait for a few days or weeks between tests because only one set of allergens can be tested at a time. This method is not very effective in identifying allergies to foods. Since it is not normal to inject foods under the skin, it is not surprising that there usually isn't a significant reaction.

11. Provocative/Neutralizing Technique

This test evaluates cellular immunity by determining patient response to the intradermal injection or topical application of one or more antigens. A minute amount of allergen (a weak dilution) is injected skin deep. It is strong enough to provoke the allergic symptoms in a person. The dilution and the amount of allergen used are noted. The allergen can produce skin erythema and/or wheal around the injected site. A record is kept of the amount, dilution and time injected. After a period of time, the size and shape of the wheal is observed. If the patient feels any reaction (dizzy spells, nausea, etc.), the tester will inject a smaller dose (weaker dilution) of the allergen that is capable of neutralizing the provocative action. This usually takes away the unpleasant symptoms or allergic reactions the patient felt from the initial injection. This is called the neutralizing dose. The neutralizing dose is used to relieve the allergic symptom and keep the patient under control for days.

12. Intradermal Test

The intradermal test is considered to be more accurate for food allergies than a plain scratch test. The name comes from the fact that a small portion of the extract of the allergen is injected intradermally, between the superficial layers of skin. Many people who show no reaction to the dermal or scratch type of testing show positive results when the same allergens are applied intradermally.

As in scratch tests, some patients can go into anaphylactic shock when extremely allergic items are injected into the body. The painful procedure can cause soreness for several days. The patient must wait a few days or weeks between tests, because only one set of allergens can be tested at a time.

13. Radioallergosorbant Test (RAST)

The radio-allergosorbant test or RAST measures IgE antibodies in serum by radioimmunoassay and identifies specific allergens causing allergic reactions. In this test, a sample of patient's serum is exposed to a panel of allergen particle complexes (APCs) on cellulose disks. Radiolabeled anti-IgE antibody is then added. This binds to the IgE-APC complexes. After centrifugation, the amount of radioactivity in the particular material is directly proportional to the amount of IgE antibodies present. Test results are compared with control values and represent the patient's reactivity to a specific allergen.

14. ELIZA

Another blood serum test for allergies is called the "ELIZA" (enzyme-linked immuno-zorbent assay) test. In this test, blood serum is tested for various immunoglobulin and their concentrations. Previous exposure to the allergen is necessary for this test to be positive in the case of an allergy. Eliza can identify an antibody or antigen, and replaces or supplements radioimmunoassay and immunofluorescence. To measure a specific antibody, an antigen is fixed to a solid phase medium, incubated with a serum sample. Then it is incubated with an anti-immunoglobulin-tagged enzyme. The excess unbound enzyme is washed from the system and a substrate is added. Hydrolysis of the substrate produces a color change, quantified by a spectrophotometer. The amount of antigen or antibody in the serum sample can then be measured. This method is safe, sensitive, and simple to perform and provides reproducible results. For this test to show some positive results the patient must be exposed to particular foods within a certain amount of time. If the patient has never been exposed to certain foods, the test results may be unsatisfactory.

15. EMF Test (Electro Magnetic Field Test)

The electromagnetic component of the human energy field can be detected with simple muscle response testing. The pool of electromagnetic energy around an object or a person allows the energy exchange. Human field absorbs the energy from the nearby object and processes through the network of nerve energy pathways. If the foreign energy field shares suitable charges with the human energy field, the human field absorbs the foreign energy for its advantage and becomes stronger. If the foreign energy field carries unsuitable charges, the human energy field causes repulsion from the foreign energy field. These types of reactions of the human field can be determined by testing an indicator muscle (specific muscle) before and during contact with an allergen. The electro- magnetic field of the humans or the human vibrations can also be measured by using the sophisticated electronic equipment developed by Dr. Valerie Hunt, Malibu, California. This genius researcher, a retired UCLA professor of physics, has proven her theory of the Science of Human Vibrations through 25 years of extensive research and clinical studies. Her book, "Infinite Mind" explains it all.

16. Sublingual Test

Another prevalent allergy test, which is used by clinical ecologists and some nutritionists, is called a sublingual test. It involves the instillation of a tiny amount of allergen extract under the tongue. If the test is positive, symptoms may appear very rapidly. The symptoms may include dramatic mental and behavioral reactions in addition to physical reactions. Some kinesiologists also use sublingual testing, but only for food items. A tiny amount of the food substance is placed under the tongue, and the patient is checked by muscle response testing.

17. Cytotoxic Testing

Cytotoxic testing is a form of blood test that was developed a few years ago. Many nutritionally oriented practitioners use this test. In this method, an extract of the allergic substance is mixed with a sample of the person's blood. It is then observed under the microscope for changes in white cells. Since foods and other allergic substances do not normally get into the blood in this manner, cytotoxic testing does not give reliable results.

20. Pulse Testing

Pulse testing is another simple way of determining food allergy. This test was developed by Arthur Coca M.D., in the 1950's. Research has shown that if you are allergic to something and you eat it, your pulse rate speeds up.

Step 1: Establish your baseline pulse by counting radial pulse at the wrist for a full minute.

Step 2: Put a small portion of the suspected allergen in the mouth, preferably under the tongue. Taste the substance for two minutes. Do not swallow any portion of it. The taste will send the signal to the brain, which will send a signal through the sympathetic nervous system to the rest of the body.

Step 3: Re-take the pulse with the allergen still in the mouth. An increase or decrease in pulse rate of 10% or more is considered an allergic reaction. The greater the degree of allergy the greater the difference in the pulse rate.

This test is useful to test food allergies. If you are allergic to very many foods and if you consume a few allergens at the same time, it will be hard to detect the exact allergen causing the reaction just by this test.

21. Blood Pressure Test

This test is similar to the pulse test. Systolic blood pressure reading is checked for changes in reading before and after the contact with the allergen.

Step 1: Establish your baseline by checking the systolic blood pressure.

Step 2: Put a small amount of the suspected allergen in the mouth, preferably under the tongue. Taste the substance for two minutes. Do not swallow any portion of it. The taste will send the signal to the brain, which will send a signal through the sympathetic nervous system to the rest of the body.

Step 3: Re-take the systolic blood pressure with the allergen still in the mouth. An increase in systolic blood pressure rate of 10% or more is considered an allergic reaction. The greater the degree of allergy the higher the blood pressure change will be.

22. The Elimination Diet

The elimination diet, which was developed by Dr. Albert H. Rowe of Oakland, California, consists of a very limited diet that must be followed for a period long enough to determine whether or not any of the foods included in it are responsible for the allergic symptoms. If a fruit allergy is suspected, for example, all fruits are eliminated from the diet for a specific period, which may vary from a few days to several weeks, depending on the severity of the symptoms. For patients who have suffered allergic symptoms over a period of several years, it is sometimes necessary to abstain from the offending foods for several weeks before the symptoms subside. Therefore, the importance of adhering strictly to the diet during the diagnostic period is very important. When the patient has been free of symptoms for a specific period, other foods are added, one at a time, until a normal diet is attained.

23. Rotation Diet

Another way to test for food allergy is through a "rotation diet," in which a different group of food is eaten every day for a week. In this method seven groups of food are eaten each week, with something different each day. The rotation starts again the following Monday. This way, reactions to any group can be traced and can be eliminated. All of these diets work better for people who are less reactive. The inherent danger in any of these methods is clear: If you are highly allergic to a certain food item you can become very sick if you eat that particular food during testing even if you have not touched it for years.

24. Like Cures Like

There are other allergy treatment methods in practice. Homeopaths believe that if an allergen is introduced to the patient in minute concentrations at various times, the patient can build up enough antibodies toward that particular antigen. Eventually, the patient's violent reactions to that particular substance may reduce in intensity. In some cases, reactions may subside completely and the patient can use or eat the item without any adverse reaction.

25. Urine Therapy

The theory behind giving the urine shots (injection) and own blood serum shots work similarly. A patient is asked to eat a particular suspected allergen at different intervals in a day. The urine of that person is collected after several hours and injected into the body. When a person eats a certain substance, the body creates antibodies for that substance, that are excreted in the urine. This urine is injected into the person, and his own antibodies are introduced into the body as an injectant. This supposedly builds up more antibodies, and the theory holds that the allergic person eventually will not react violently toward the allergen.

26. Blood Sample Injection

The same idea is applied when injecting one's own blood sample intramuscularly. When you suffer from any autoimmune disorder, you create many antibodies in your body. The body creates special antibodies to fight its problems. A sample of blood is taken (about 2 cubic centimeter) and injected into the person, (his/her own antibodies are re-introduced into the body as an injectant). This supposedly builds up more antibodies, and the theory holds that an allergic person eventually will not react violently toward the allergens.

27. Sit With The Allergen In Your Palm

NAET patients are taught to test the allergen in another easy and safe way. Place a small portion of the suspected allergen in a baby food jar and ask the person to hold in her/his palm touching with the fingertips of the same hand for 15 minutes to 30 minutes. An allergic person will begin to feel uneasy when holding the allergen in his/her palm for a while giving rise to various unpleasant symptoms: begin to get hot, itching, hives, irregularities in heart beats (fast or slow heart beats), nausea, light headedness, etc. Since the allergen is inside the glass bottle, when such uncomfortable sensation is felt, the allergen can be put away immediately and hands washed to remove the energy of the allergen from the fingertips. This should stop the reactions immediately. In this way, the patient can detect out the allergens easily.

All of the above methods work on a certain percentage of people. Curiously, people who had undergone all of these treatments were still found to be allergic to their identified allergies when they were tested again by muscle response testing. They still had to be treated by NAET to make them non-reactive.

CHAPTER FOUR

IS IT REALLY ADHD?

4

IS IT REALLY ADHD?

HOW DO WE DIAGNOSE ADHD?

The diagnostic process for ADHD, must begin with a formal medical history. Most people are interested in understanding the differences and/or the similarities of the methods of diagnosis, the effectiveness and length of treatment between traditional western medicine and oriental medicine. Since the purpose of this book is to provide information about the new treatment method of NAET, more attention will be given to oriental medicine and NAET.

The American Psychiatric Association periodically publishes an updated manual of diagnostic criteria for various mental conditions and behavioral abnormalities. The most recent edition, as of this writing is the *Diagnostic and Statistical Manual 1V (DSM 1V)*. It includes guidelines for diagnosis of attention deficit disorder. DSM 1V is for experienced professionals and is not intended for self-diagnosis of attention deficit disorder or any other condition described in the manual.

WHAT ARE THE SIGNS OF ADHD?

Professionals, who diagnose ADHD, use the diagnostic criteria set forth by the American Psychiatric Association (1994), in *The Diagnostic and Statistical Manual of Mental Disorders, DSM-1V* released in 1994.

According to DSM-1V the most obvious signs associated with this disorder are inattentiveness (short attention span, failure to listen, failure to follow instructions, inability to finish projects and stay focused); impulsiveness (acting before thinking, answering before completely listening to the question, etc.); and hyperactivity (excessive activity, fidgeting, inability to stay seated, running, climbing, moving back and forth all the time, etc.). A child can have any one of these symptoms alone or in combination with two, more or all of the above.

In addition to these problems, depending on the child's age and developmental stage, parents and teachers may see temper tantrums, frustration, anger, bossiness, difficulty in following rules, disorganization, social rejection, low-self esteem, poor academic achievement, and inadequate self-application.

There are many books written on this subject of ADHD and every book you read will give you all the standard criteria or diagnostic guidelines to detect and diagnose ADHD. So I am not going into details about diagnosing an ADHD child or adult through standard criteria in this book. But I am going to spend some time explaining things that you absolutely need to understand to recognize this health disorder, so that you can look for appropriate help.

THE BEST DIAGNOSTIC TOOL

A detailed clinical history is the best diagnostic tool for any medical condition.

It is extremely important for the patient or his/her parents or guardians to cooperate with the physician in giving all possible information about the child to the doctor in order to obtain the best results. It is my hope that this chapter will help bring about a clearer understanding between NAET specialists and their patients; because, in order to obtain the most satisfactory results, both parties must work together as a team.

The doctor should gather a detailed history of the child before formulating a diagnosis of ADHD. Your doctor's office may ask you to complete a relevant questionnaire during your first appointment. It is important to cooperate with the office staff and provide as accurate history as possible.

THE ADHD PATIENT-QUESTIONNAIRE

Prenatal history (socio-economic factors, exposures to substance abuse, cadmium, lead, mercury, coffee, alcohol, chemical toxins, carbon monoxide poisoning, bacterial toxins, emotional traumas during fetal development), delivery, birth records including birth weight and APGAR scores.

Growth and Developmental History

⇒ **Illnesses during early infancy?**
♦ Colic——
♦ Constipation——
♦ Diarrhea——
♦ Feeding problem——
♦ Excessive Vomiting———

- Excessive white coating on the tongue ——
- Excessive crying ——
- Poor sleep ——
- Disturbed sleep ——
- Frequent ear infection ——
- Frequent fever ——
- Immunizations——
- Response to the immunizations ——
- Common childhood diseases like measles, chickenpox, mumps, strep-throat, etc.——
- Any other unusual events (fire in the house, accidents, earthquakes, etc).——

Developmental Milestones
⇒ **Age of the child:**
- Walked alone——
- Talked——
- Toilet trained for bladder and bowel——
- Enrolled in school——

⇒ **Medical History**
- Surgeries—
- Hospitalizations——
- Diseases—
- Allergies—
- Frequent colds—
- Fevers—
- Ear infections—
- Asthma—
- Hives——
- Bronchitis—
- Pneumonia—
- Seizures—
- Sinusitis—
- Headaches—
- Vomiting ——
- Diarrhea ——
- Current medication—
- Any reaction to medication ——

♦ Antibiotics and drugs taken —
♦ Parasitic infestation —
♦ Visited other countries —

⇒ **Social History:**

♦ **Learning:** grades at school, interaction between friends and teachers, interaction between family members, activities at school, phobias, and problems with discipline.
♦ **Behaviors:** cooperative, uncooperative, disruptive and/or aggressive behaviors; overactive, restless, inattentive, day dreams; uncooperative with his/her peers and adults; incomplete or sloppy work.
♦ **Habits:** temper tantrums, excessively active, constantly moving in seat or room, low self esteem, short attention span, poor memory, unusual fears, falls down often, clumsy, and unintentionally drops things.
♦ **Hobbies:** reading, painting, singing, and horse back riding, etc.

⇒ **Family History**
    The medical history of the immediate relatives, mother, father, and siblings should be noted. The same questions are asked about the patient's relatives: grandparents, aunts, uncles, and cousins. A tendency to get sick or have allergies is not always inherited directly from the parents. It may skip generations or manifest in nieces or nephews rather than in direct descendants.

⇒ **Questions are also asked about :**
    Alcoholism, drug abuse, mental disorders, and other health disorders. The careful NAET specialist will also determine whether or not diseases such as tuberculosis, cancer, diabetes, rheumatic or glandular disorders exist, or have ever occurred in the patient's family history. All of these facts help give the NAET specialist a more complete picture of the hereditary characteristics of the patient. A *tendency* is inherited. It may be manifested differently in different people. Unlike the tendency, an actual medical condition such as ADHD is not always inherited. Parents may have had can-

cer or rheumatism, but the child can manifest that allergic inheritance as ADHD.

⇒ **Present history:**

When the family history is complete, the practitioner will need to look into the history of the patient's chief complaint and its progression. Some typical preliminary questions include: "When did your child's first symptom occur?" Did you notice your child's problem when he/she was an infant or a child, or did you first notice the symptoms during adolescence, or fully grown? Did it occur after going through a certain procedure? For example, did it occur for the first time after a dental procedure like a root canal, the first antibiotic treatment or after installing a water filter? Did it occur after acquiring a waterbed, tricycle or after a booster dose of immunization or vaccination? One of my patients reported that her son's ADD began a few months after he received a booster dose of DPT.

Once a careful history is taken, the practitioner often discovers that the patient's first symptoms occurred in early childhood. He or she may have suffered from infantile eczema, or asthma, but never associated it with ADD, which may not have appeared until a later age.

Next, the doctor will want to know the circumstances surrounding and immediately preceding the first symptoms. Typical questions will include: "Did you change the child's diet or put him/her on a special diet? Did he/she eat something that he/she hadn't eaten lately, (perhaps for two or three months)? Did you feed him/her one type of food repeatedly, every day for a few days? Did the symptoms follow a childhood illness, (whooping cough, measles, chicken pox, diphtheria) or any immunization for such an illness? Did they follow some other illness such as influenza, pneumonia or a major operation? Did the problem begin after your vacation to an island, to another country, or after an insect bite? When did the first symptom appear?

Any one of these factors can be responsible for triggering a severe allergic manifestation or precipitate the first noticeable symptoms of an allergic condition. Therefore, it is very important to obtain full and accurate answers when taking the patient's medical history.

Other important questions relate to the frequency and occurrence of the attacks. Although foods may be a factor, if the symptoms occur only at specific times of the year, the trouble most likely is due to pollens. Often a patient is sensitive to certain foods but has a natural tolerance that prevents sickness until the pollen sensitivity adds sufficient allergens to throw the body into an imbalance. If symptoms occur only on specific days of the week, they are probably due to something contacted or eaten on that particular day.

The causes of ADD/ADHD in different patients can, at first, appear random. Regular attacks of mental irritability was caused in one patient after he read the Sunday newspaper. The ink caused a severe allergic reaction. Another patient reacted similarly to the comic section of the newspaper. A man always had a severe tension headache every Sunday morning. The cause was traced to eating a traditional spinach dish every Saturday night with his family. He was allergic to the spinach in the food. Still another patient had an allergic attack of sneezing, runny nose, mental irritability, and headaches on Saturdays. I traced the allergy to the chemical compounds in a lotion she used to set her hair with on Friday afternoons.

The time of day when the attacks occur is also of importance in determining the cause of an allergic manifestation. If it always occurs before mealtime hypoglycemia may be a possible cause. If

§

it occurs after meals, an allergy to carbohydrates and starch complexes or something in the meal should be suspected. If it occurred regularly at night, it is quite likely that there is something in the bedroom that is aggravating the condition. It may be that the patient is sensitive to: feathers in the pillow or comforter, wood cabinets, marble floors, carpets, side tables, end tables, bed sheets, pillows, pillow cases, detergents used in washing clothes, indoor plants, shrubs, trees, or grasses outside the patient's window. One of my patients suffered from severe insomnia and irritability at night. After spending a few minutes in bed, he regularly got up agitated and uptight and spend rest of the night without sleep. He was found to be allergic to his blue colored silk bed sheet and pillow cases; he was found to be allergic to the color blue, which instead of calming him, made him agitated and irritable.

Many patients react violently to house dust, different types of furniture, polishes, house plants, tap water and purified water. Most of the city water suppliers change the water chemicals only once or twice a year. Although, this is done with good intentions, people with chemical allergies may get sicker if they ingest the same chemicals over and over for months or years. Contrary to traditional western thinking, developing immunity can be the exception rather than the rule.

Occasionally, switching the chemicals around gives allergic patients a change of allergens and a chance for them to recover from the existing reactions. In this way, repeated use of the same chemicals can be avoided.

Across the United States, chlorination is used as the primary disinfectant in water systems. Although chlorination will kill most of the bacteria, viruses are not destroyed by any of these cleansing processes. Tri-halomethanes, which are a by-product of chlorine, are also used to clean the water. Ozone is used as a disinfectant for drinking water. Some of these chemicals are known to cause birth defects, nervous system disorders, damage to body organs and many other irreversible sicknesses.

The doctor should ask the patient to make a daily log of all the foods he/she is eating. The ingredients in the food should be checked for possible allergens. Certain common allergens like corn products, MSG (monosodium glutamate or Accent), citric acid, etc., are used in food preparations.

Allergy to corn is one of today's most common allergies, especially in ADHD patients. Unfortunately, cornstarch is found in almost every processed food and some toiletries and drugs too. Chinese food, baking soda, baking powder, and toothpaste contain large amounts of cornstarch. It is the binding product in almost all vitamins and pills, including aspirin and Tylenol. Corn syrup is the natural sweetener in many of the products we ingest, including soft drinks. Corn silk is found in cosmetics and corn oil is used as a vegetable oil. For sensitive people this food adds another nightmare.

Other common ingredients in many preparations that ADHD people may react severely to are the various gums (acacia gum, xanthine gum, karaya gum, etc.). Numerous gums are used in candy bars, yogurt, cream cheese, soft drinks, soy sauce, barbecue sauce, fast food products, macaroni and cheese, etc.

Carob, a staple in many health food products, is another item that causes brain irritability among allergic people. Many health-conscious people are turning to natural food products in which carob is used as a chocolate and cocoa substitute. It is also used as a natural coloring or stiffening agent in soft drinks, cheeses, sauces, etc. We discovered that some of the causes of "holiday flu" and suicidal attempts are allergies to carob, chocolate, and turkey.

When assessing a child in whom ADHD is suspected, care must be taken not to misdiagnose him/her. Misdiagnosis of ADHD can probably hurt the child and his family's peace of mind for a long time.

As I have stated earlier, in my opinion, the majority of people that are labelled as having ADHD are not suffering from ADHD. They may be suffering from simple undiagnosed allergies.

If a child is suffering from any of the symptoms described in the diagnostic criteria for ADHD it may not necessarily mean that he/she is absolutely suffering from ADHD. Many food and environmental allergic symptoms overlap or mimic variety of diseases including many neurological and brain disorders.

After completing the patient's history, the NAET specialist should examine the patient for the usual vital signs. A physical examination is performed to check for any abnormal growth or condition. If the patient has an area of discomfort in the body, it should be inspected. It is important to note the type and area of discomfort and its relationship to an acupuncture point. Most pain and discomfort in the body usually occurs around some important acupuncture point.

Twelve meridians combined with their channels and branches cover almost every part of the human body. The NAET specialist should examine all these meridians and branches for possible energy blockages. An acupuncturist is trained to understand the exact location of the pathways of these meridians. For this reason, the exact symptoms are very important. By identifying the symptoms, you can identify the area of the energy blockage. From this location, the experienced acupuncturist/ NAET specialist can detect the meridians, organs, muscles and nerve roots associated with the blockage. The NAET specialist will then be able to make an appropriate diagnosis by evaluating the presenting symptoms (read

Chapter 7 for possible pathological symptoms) and determine what particular allergen is causing the specific problem. When the source of the problem is identified, treatment becomes easier.

CHAPTER FIVE

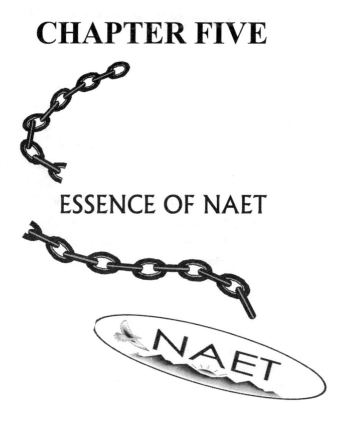

ESSENCE OF NAET

5

ESSENCE OF NAET

The word "kinesiology" refers to the science of movement. It was first proposed in 1964 by Dr. George Goodheart, a Detroit doctor of chiropractic medicine. As a function of his practice, Dr. Goodheart learned a great deal about a patient's condition by using isolated movements of various muscles. Isolation techniques—a chiropractic procedure, made it possible to test the strength of an individual muscle or muscle group without the help of other muscles. Dr. Goodheart, with the help of Dr. Hetrick and others concluded after many experiments, that structural imbalance causes disorganization of the entire body. This disorganization results in specific disorders of the glands, organs and central nervous system. His findings were similar to what pioneer Chinese doctors also had observed.

Kinesiology holds that when the body is disorganized, the structural balance or electrical force is not functioning normally. When that happens, the electrical energy–life force doesn't flow freely through the nerve cells and causes energy blockages in the person. According to the Chinese, the free flow of energy is necessary for the normal functioning of the body. When your flow of energy gets blocked, you become ill. The messages both from and to the brain also pass through this energy channel. The energy and the messages travel from cell to cell in nanoseconds.

Many years ago, pioneer Chinese doctors and philosophers had studied these energy pathways and networks of the human body energy system by observing living people and their normal and abnormal body functions. The Chinese had learned to manipulate these energy pathways, or meridians, to the body's advantage. About 4,000 years ago, there was no scientific equipment available to feel or observe the presence of the energy flow and its pathways. Now, it is possible to study and trace the energy flows and pathways by using Kirlian photography and radioactive tracer isotopes. Although the existence of energy pathways in the human body has only been confirmed relatively recently, the Chinese doctors hypothesized and established their existence long ago.

Chinese medical theory points out that free-flow of Chi through the meridians is necessary to keep the body in perfect balance. In the United States during the 19th century, the founder of Chiropractic medicine, Daniel David Palmer, said, "Too much or too little energy is sickness." Even though it is believed that Palmer may have had no knowledge of Chinese medicine, his theory corresponded with the ancient Chinese theory of "free flow of energy."

In late 1800's, American chiropractic medicine developed under Dr. D. D. Palmer. Through him, doctors of chiropractic learned about the importance of stabilizing energy and manipulating the spinal segments and nerve roots to keep them perfectly aligned, bringing the body to a balanced state. In the East, acupuncture developed based on the ancient Chinese theory. Eastern acupuncturists tried to bring balance by manipulating the energy meridians at various acupuncture points, inserting needles to remove blockages and reinstating the "free flow of Chi" along the energy pathways. East and West, unaware of each other's findings, worked in a similar manner toward the same goal: to balance the energy and to free sick people from their pain.

Both groups realized that the overflow or underflow of energy, or in other words, too much or too little energy is the cause of an imbalance. When the flow is reinstated, the balance is restored.

HOW CAN YOU REMOVE THE CAUSE OF BLOCKAGE?

A trained acupuncturist can differentiate between the overflow and underflow of Chi, and its affected meridians and organs. When treatment is administered to strengthen the under flowing or hypo-functioning organ, while draining the overflowing meridians and the organs, balance is achieved faster. This is the practice of acupuncture. NTT and NAET are built on acupuncture theory, but have taken it one step further. Using the ideas from acupuncture theory, without using actual needle insertion, meridians can be unblocked, overflowing meridians can be drained and the excess energy can be rerouted through the empty meridians and associated organs. Thus the entire body reaches homeostasis. NAET is perhaps the missing link that various professionals have been searching for years. NTT and NAET will be discussed in detail in later chapters.

When the body senses a danger or a threat from an allergen, sensory nerves carry the message to the brain and the brain will alert the whole body about the imminent danger. Muscles contract to conserve energy, other defense forces like lymph, blood cells, etc., get ready to face the emergency. Spinal nerves also get tightened due to the contracted muscles. Vertebrae go into misalignment causing impingement at the affected vertebral level. Energy is blocked due to the impingement. So, a good chiropractic adjustment can remove the nerve impingement at the specific vertebral level and this can unblock the blocked energy pathway making the energy circulate again freely.

Herbs can cause similar healing. Electromagnetic forces of special herbs actually have the ability to enter selective energy pathways and push energy blockages out of the body to restore the energy balance. A well-trained herbologist can bring about the same result as an NAET specialist. Chiropractic, kinesiology, acupuncture and herbology are blended together to create NAET.

Brain chemicals are not produced or distributed correctly in ADD and ADHD patients. If given a chance, appropriate stimulation to the spinal nerves, the brain and nervous system can produce substances within the body and distribute them appropriately including adrenaline, thyroxin, pituitropin, serotonin, dopamine, endorphin, dynorphin, enkephalin, interferon, cytokines, interleukin, leukotriene, prostaglandin, and other immune mediators to heal many problems. The brain has the ability to create appropriate remedial secretions that release to the target tissue and organs when needed to heal infections, allergies, imbalances, and immune deficiency diseases, etc., as long as the brain receives the right directions and commands. This has been demonstrated repeatedly and proven in many cases when treated with NAET.

According to western medical researchers, the actual cause of ADHD is not known. Scientific evidence suggests that in many cases, the disorder is genetically transmitted, results from a chemical imbalance and/or an allergy, or a deficiency in certain neurotransmitters. These are chemicals that help the brain regulate behavior. A study conducted by the National Institute of Mental Health showed that the rate at which the brain uses glucose, its main energy source, is lower in subjects with ADHD than in subjects without ADHD (Zametkin et al." 1990).

When body functions do not take place freely, the body begins to succumb to health problems: fatigue, headaches, sleep disturbances, irritability, forgetfulness, confusion, depression, cravings, eating disorders, difficulty in thinking, poor concentration, phobias, crying spells, suicidal thoughts, feelings of loneliness even in crowds, burning sensations on the skin and on the limbs (hands, feet, palms and soles). Most of these symptoms are experienced by ADHD patients.

If you fail to eliminate the blockage immediately, the adverse energy eventually takes over the body and causes problems at deeper levels. For example, the headaches can turn into irritability, hyperactivity, and other brain disorders; neuropsychological complaints such as anger, irritability, confusion, and depression, etc., may turn the sufferer into a psychiatric case, possibly leading to institutionalization.

We treated a 28-year-old computer programmer who began to feel extreme fatigue, irritability, depression, and mood swings, a year after he started working with a well-known computer firm. He had a wife and two children. When he started experiencing incapacitating exhaustion, he began dreading his work. His output also started to slow down. He was diagnosed as having "chronic fatigue syndrome." His energy was drained to the point that he was unable to walk without assistance. Finally, he had to file for disability insurance. His health improved when he was away from work for a while. Once he returned to work, his problems started all over—even though he was given regular physical therapy and supportive treatments.

After four years of illness, he came to our office and it was discovered that he was highly allergic to plastic products and his computer keyboard. He was also allergic to computer radiation.

After he was treated by NAET for plastics, keyboard, and radiation, he was able to resume his regular work.

NAET treatment works with the entire body: the physical body (organs, brain, nervous system and tissues), physiological body (circulation of blood, fluids and nerve energy) and emotional body (mind, thoughts and spirituality). It helps to detoxify the system by clearing the adverse energies of the allergens from the entire body. Thus it enables the body to relax, absorb and assimilate appropriate nutrients from the food that once caused allergies and support the proper growth of the entire body.

The human nervous system controls every function of every system in the body. This complicated maze of nerves is still not completely understood. Some basic knowledge about the human nervous system will help you to understand the relationship between the human body and allergies. More importantly, it opens the door of knowledge to the concepts that lead to the treatment of allergies and allergy related diseases. It allows you to make readjustments to the nervous system rather than having to depend on a lifetime of allergy shots, antihistamines, and various extensive, expensive types of allergy treatments.

The nervous system is without a doubt the most complex, widely investigated and least understood system in the body known to man. Its structures and activities are interwoven with every aspect of our lives: physical, cultural and intellectual. Accordingly, investigators of many different disciplines, all holding their own methodologies, motivations, and persuasions, converge in its study. Depending on the context, there are many appropriate ways of embarking upon a study of the nervous system.

For purposes of understanding the relationship between the human body and the nervous system, it is essential to look at some of the structures and functions of the nervous system that are both directly or indirectly involved in the adaptation process. This section will not cover the structural aspects of the human nervous system, such as the location of nerve ganglions, trunks, cells, endings, etc.; rather, you are urged to refer to appropriate sections in Gray's or other anatomy texts for such information. In this section, we will try to enlighten you on the chemical and electrical energy aspects only.

The central nervous system consists of the brain and the spinal cord. The peripheral nervous system consists of all of the nerves that leave the spinal cord and go to muscles and various parts of the body. This includes the motor and sensory nerves that are responsible not only for muscle movements of the body, but also for carrying the sensations of heat, cold and touch from various parts of the body to the spinal cord. The autonomic nervous system consists of the sympathetic and parasympathetic nervous systems, which are composed of the nerves regulating the functions of various vital smooth muscle organs such as the heart, liver, and brain, etc.

One of the primary functions of the human nervous system is gathering and processing of information. As the total human being consciously senses and responds according to the stimuli presented by the environment, millions of minor adjustments are constantly being made automatically without our conscious decision-making. For instance, when you are hot, you consciously move yourself away from the sun, or turn on the air conditioning. But the body is already unconsciously making several hundred minor adjustments that trigger changes in the blood flow and the heart rate, expanding and contracting the blood vessels near the skin surfaces, activating the lymph glands, turning on the sweat glands, and so on. These actions of the autonomic nervous system are reprogrammed into the very cells of the body that respond to conscious activity. The autonomic responses are constantly readjusting to respond appropriately to the changing environment.

It is extremely important to recognize the body's attempts to maintain a homeostatic state (balance within the organism). The total balance takes place in various steps, utilizing assistance from a number of functional units. These functional units are large bodies of tissues composed of many microscopic cells, each having a specialized job in the body. These special tissues provide assistance in creating homeostasis at the lowest levels within the individual's cells themselves.

The process through which this occurs is very complex, requiring considerable understanding of the biochemical and bioelectrical properties of the cells. Simplified, it can be said that all cells are surrounded by a plasma membrane similar to a microscopic plastic bag. The walls of this membrane are thick enough to contain the intracellular materials while maintaining the cell shape and size. It is also strong enough to protect the cells from invasion of the intracellular materials that surround each and every cell.

Conversely, it is thin enough and permeable enough to allow the free flow of nutrients. The ionic or magnetic properties of the atoms that make up the fluids inside the cell differ from the fluids surrounding the cells. Because of the differences in ionic composition, it follows that there are differences in their electrical properties. The disparity in electrical energies can be measured in laboratory experiments on various kinds of tissues. But more importantly, it can assess the individual cell's responses to the electrical charges, which add up to millions of measurements per minute.

As a stimulus is applied on some point on the organism, it sets up a sequence of events that is eventually transmitted to the surfaces of the excitable cells, which in turn redistributes the ions across the surface. This becomes a transient, reversible wave of change which presumably affects the permeability of cell membranes, allowing fluids to penetrate. The transfer of fluids changes the cell shape, size and function until it turns back to its original or homeostatic state.

In some primitive multicellular and all uni-cellullar life forms, individual cells are capable of reacting to stimuli; whereas most complex life forms (that make up the processing nervous system) consist of a system of specific cells to accept and interpret stimuli. Thus, in the human body we have highly specialized receptor cells whose total function is to receive stimuli. These receptor cells work in accord with neurons (nerve cells), for the integration and conduction of information; the effector cells (the contractile and glandular cells) operate the action of the responses.

This is the foundational premise upon which the understanding of allergies is based; the muscle response testing detects allergies and NAET eliminates allergies.

The ends of various dendrites and axons do not connect together to create a wire link; rather, they are interlaced, without touching. The space between the ends of the threadlike axons and dendrites are called synapses. The electrical impulses, or energy impulses, jump these spaces in their journey to the brain and back.

Enzymes, on the surface of the neurons act as mediators (like cholinesterase) and complete the circuit. These enzymes are known as neurotransmitters and are extremely important in making intercommunication possible among the cells, neurons, tissues, organs and different body parts. These neurotransmitters vary among neurons, depending upon the specificity of tissue. Although vastly different in chemical composition, all these enzymes share a common origin. They are produced by the neurons, then released into the synapses as the nerve impulse arrives.

The actions and neurological functions of these enzymes in our bodies are still not completely understood, primarily because of the wide distribution of such enzymes throughout the body. These enzymes include mono-amino acids, known as nor-adrenalin, serotonin, histamines, (all of which have an excitatory affect on the body's nervous system) and dopamine, which has an inhibitory effect.

The ability of the central nervous system to react almost instantaneously to a stimulus (such as the sensation of heat, cold, smell, etc.), even on the most remote part of the extremities, is probably the result of the common origin of the nervous system. The body is made up of trillions of individually well-equipped cells. Each cell has the memory to reproduce any number of chemicals and functions in the body. For some reason, in ADHD patients, some of these cells remain dormant or have lost the memory to reproduce the neurochemicals (appropriate neuro-transmitters) temporarily. Due to the inactive chemical messengers, messages do not transfer appropriately to the other neurons. So their nervous system does not work smoothly as a normal person's nervous system.

If the stimulus reaches the brain (providing it is not short-circuited by nerve damage, blockage, or missed chemical response due to some defect in the neurotransmitters), the brain accepts the message. It then formulates and transmits a response to all other receptors in the body. In turn, the receptors receive the message as either harmful or harmless. If the receptors receive the message as harmful, they repel it and confirm their findings to the brain. If more stimuli with negative reactions reach the brain, the brain accepts the rejection message from the majority of receptors. Since the brain's responses are impartial, the receptors corresponding to the area of the stimuli will react accordingly, setting in motion evasive actions. In the worst case scenario, where the body cannot effectively avoid or reject the stimulus, it will set up a reaction in an effort to cleanse the body of the stimulus. In an ADHD person, incorrect or incomplete stimulus reaches the brain repeatedly and as a result an inappropriate response is set forth.

Activities of the sympathetic system prepare the body for increased activities. Biochemically, the action of the sympathetic system is characterized by the formation of nor-adrenaline and adrenaline (along with some other basic enzymes) to prepare the body for reaction.

Chiropractors and acupuncturists are stimulating the sympathetic nerve activity, removing the nerve energy blockages to reinstate the nerve energy circulation in the body. These two groups of medical practitioners from East and West have learned to manipulate the sympathetic nerves to the patient's advantage and promote healing power within the body itself without the introduction of foreign chemicals.

Beyond this point, the nervous system becomes a matter of complicated medical study. It is sufficient to say, however, that even a very minor stimulus sensed by any receptor nerve cell located on the body, will set in motion the manufacturing process of hundreds of different kinds of chemicals. Each assists the nerves in producing appropriate responses to the particular stimulus.

CHAPTER SIX

MRT TO DETECT ADHD

6

MUSCLE RESPONSE TESTING

Muscle response testing is one of the tools used by the NAET specialists to test the imbalances in the body. The same muscle response test can also be used to detect various allergens that cause imbalances in the body.

When the allergen's incompatible electromagnetic energy comes close to a person's energy field, repulsion takes place. Without recognizing this repulsive action, we frequently go near allergens (whether they are foods, drinks, chemicals, environmental substances, animals or humans) and interact with their energies. This causes energy blockages in the meridians. These blockages cause imbalances in the body. The imbalances cause illness, which creates disorganization in body function. The disorganization of the body and its function involve the vital organs, their associated muscle groups and nerve roots giving rise to brain disorders.

To prevent the allergen from causing further disarray after producing the initial blockage, the brain sends messages to every cell of the body to reject the presence of the allergen. This rejection will appear as repulsion, and the repulsion will produce different symptoms related to the affected organs.

Your body has an amazing way of telling you when you are in trouble. As a matter of habit, you often have to be hurting severely before you look for help. If you went for help at the earliest hint of need, you would save yourself from unnecessary pain and agony. This applies to allergies, too. If you expose your allergies before you are exposed to them, you won't have to suffer the consequences. If you understand your body, your brain and their clues, you can avoid the causes that contribute to the energy blockages and body imbalances.

When some people are near allergens (adversely charged substances), they receive various clues from the brain, such as: an itchy throat, watery eyes, sneezing attacks, coughing spells, unexplained pain anywhere in the body, yawning, sudden tiredness, etc. You can demonstrate the changes in the weaknesses of the muscles by testing a strong indicator muscle in the absence of an allergen and then in its presence. The muscle will stay strong without any allergen in its electro-magnetic field, but will weaken in the presence of an allergen. This response of the muscle can be used to your advantage to demonstrate the presence of an allergen near you.

MUSCLE RESPONSE TESTING

(See Illustrations of Muscle Response Testing on the Following Pages).

Muscle response testing can be preformed in the following ways:

1. Standard muscle response test can be done in standing, sitting or lying positions. You need two people to do this test: the person who is testing, the "tester," and the person being tested,

"the subject."

2. The "Oval Ring Test" can be used in testing yourself, and on a very a strong person with a strong arm. This requires only one person. If you are self-testing, you need two people: one person as tester and another as the subject.

3. Surrogate testing can be used in testing an infant, invalid person, extremely strong or very weak person, an animal, plant or a tree. The surrogate's muscle is tested by the tester, subject maintains skin-to-skin contact with the surrogate while being tested. The surrogate does not get affected by the testing. NAET treatments can also be administered through the surrogate very effectively without causing any interference with the surrogate's energy.

FIGURE 6-1
STANDARD MUSCLE RESPONSE TESTING

Two people are required to perform standard muscle response testing. The person who performs the test is called the tester, and the person who is being tested is called the subject. The subject can be tested lying down, standing or sitting. The lying-down position is the most convenient for both the tester and the subject; it also achieves more accurate results.

Step 1:   The subject lies on a firm surface with one arm raised (left arm in the picture below), 90 degrees to the body with the palm facing outward and the thumb facing toward the big toe.

Step 2:   The tester stands on the subject's (right) side. The subject's right arm is kept to his/her side with the palm either kept open to the air, or in a loose fist. The fingers should not touch any material, fabric or any part of the table the arm is resting on. This can give wrong test results. The left arm of the subject is raised 90 degrees to the body. The tester's left palm is contacting the subject's left wrist (Figure 6-1).

Step 3:   The tester using the left arm tries to push down on the subject's raised left arm toward the subject's left big toe. The subject resists the push of the tester on the arm (the indicator muscle or pre-determined muscle). The PDM remains strong if the subject is well balanced at the time of testing. It is essential to test a strong PDM to get accurate results. If the muscle or raised arm is weak and gives way under pressure without the presence of an allergen, either the subject is not balanced, or the tester is performing the test improperly; For example, the tester might be trying to overpower the subject. The subject does not need to gather up strength from other muscles in the body to resist the tester with all his/her might. Only five to 10 pounds of pressure needs to be applied on the muscle for three to five seconds. If the muscle shows weakness, the tester will be able to judge the difference with only that small amount of pressure. Much practice is needed to test and sense the differences properly. If you cannot test properly or effectively the first few times, there is no need to get discouraged or frustrated. Please remember that practice makes you perfect.

Step 4: If the indicator muscle remains strong when tested a sign that the subject is found to be balanced - then the tester should put the suspected allergen into the palm of the subject's resting hand. The sensory receptors, on the tip of the fingers, are extremely sensitive in recognizing allergens. The fingertips have specialized sensory receptors that can send messages to and from the brain.

FIGURE 6-2
MRT WITH ALLERGEN

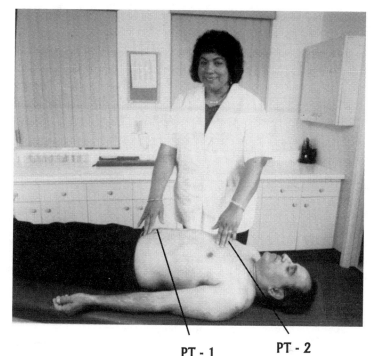

PT - 1   PT - 2

FIGURE 6-3
BALANCING THE PATIENT

When the subject's fingertips touch the allergen, the sensory receptors sense the charges of the allergen and relay the message to the brain. If it is an incompatible charge, the strong PDM will go weak. If the charges are compatible to the body, the indicator muscle will remain strong. This way, you can test any number of items to determine the compatible and incompatible charges of the items against the body.

Step 5: This step is used if the patient is found to be out of balance as indicated by the indicator muscle or raised arm presenting weak— without the presence of an allergen. The tester then places his or her fingertips of one hand at 'point 1' on the mid-line of the subject, about one and a half inches below the navel. The other hand is placed on 'point 2', in the center of the chest on the mid-line, level with the nipple line. The tester taps these two points or massages gently clockwise with the fingertips about 20 or 30 seconds, then repeats steps 2 and 3. If the indicator muscle tests strong, continue on to step 4. If the indicator muscle tests weak again, repeat this process.

Point 1:
Name of the point: **Sea Of Energy**
Location: One and a half inches below the navel, on the mid-line.
This is where the energy of the body is stored in abundance. When the body senses any danger around its energy field or when the body experiences energy blockages, the energy supply is cut short and stored here. If you tap or massage clockwise on that energy reservoir point, the energy starts bubbling up and emerges from this point.

Point 2:
Name of the point: **Energy Controller.**
Location: In the center of the chest on the midline of the

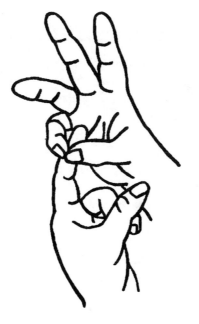

FIGURE 6-4

`O' RING TEST TO DETECT ALLERGIES

body, level with the fourth intercostal space. This is the energy dispenser unit. From this center, energy is distributed to different tissues and organs as needed. This is the point that controls and regulates the energy circulation or Chi, in the body. When the energy rises from the Sea of Energy, it goes straight to the Dominating Energy point. From here, the energy is dispersed to different meridians, organs, tissues and cells as needed to help remove the energy blockages. It does this by forcing energy circulation from inside out. During this forced energy circulation, the blockages are pushed out of the body, balancing the body's state. You sense this through the strength of the indicator muscle. Continue this procedure several times. It is very unlikely that any person will remain weak after repeating this procedure two to three times.

The 'Oval Ring Test' or 'O Ring Test' can be used in self-testing, since this requires one person to perform the test. This can also be used to test a subject, if the subject is physically very strong with a strong arm and the tester is a physically weak person.

Step 1: The tester makes an "O" shape by opposing the little finger and thumb on the same hand. Then, with the index finger of the other hand he/she tries to separate the "O" ring against pressure. If the ring separates easily, you need to use the balancing techniques as described in step 5 of the muscle response test.

Step 2: If the "O" ring remains inseparable and strong, hold the allergen in the other hand, by the fingertips, and perform step 1 again. If the "O" ring separates easily, the person is allergic to the substance he/she is touching. If the "O" ring remains strong, the substance is not an allergen.

Muscle response testing is one of the most reliable methods of allergy tests, and it is fairly easy to learn and practice in every day life. This method cuts out expensive laboratory work.

After considerable practice, some people are able to test themselves very efficiently using these methods. It is very important for allergic people to learn some form of self-testing technique to screen out contact with possible allergens to prevent allergic reactions in order to have freedom to live in this chemically polluted world. After receiving the basic 30-40 treatments from a NAET practitioner, you will be free to live wherever you like if you know how to test and avoid unexpected allergens from your surroundings. Hundreds of new allergens are thrown into the world daily by non-allergic people who do not understand the predicament of allergic people. If you want to live in this world looking and feeling normal among normal people, side by side with the allergens, you need to learn how to test on your own. It is not practical for people to treat thousands of allergens from their surroundings or go to an NAET practitioner every day for the rest of their lives. You will not be free from allergies until you learn to test accurately. It takes many hours of practice. But do not get discouraged. I have given enough information on testing methods here. You have to spend time and practice until you reach perfection.

A TIP TO MASTER SELF-TESTING

Find two items, one that you are allergic to and another that you are not, for example an apple and a banana.

You are allergic to the apple and not allergic to the banana. Hold the apple in the right hand and do the "Oval Ring Test" using your left hand. The ring easily breaks. The first few times if it didn't break, make it happen intentionally. Now hold the banana and do the same test. This time the ring doesn't break. Put the banana down, rub your hands together for 30 seconds. Take the apple and repeat the testing. Practice this every day until you can sense the difference. When you can feel the difference with these two items you can test anything around you.

SURROGATE TESTING

This method can be very useful to test and determine the allergies of an infant, a child, an invalid or disabled person, an unconscious person, an extremely strong, or very weak person, because they do not have enough muscle strength to perform an allergy test. You can also use this method to test an animal, plant, or tree.

The surrogate's muscle is tested by the tester. It is very important to remember to maintain skin-to-skin contact between the surrogate and the subject during the procedure. If you do not, then the surrogate will receive the results of testing and treatment.

NAET treatments can also be administered through the surrogate very effectively without causing any interference to the surrogate's energy. The testing or treatment does not affect surrogate as long as the subject maintains uninterrupted skin-to-skin contact with the surrogate.

As mentioned earlier, muscle response testing is one of the tools used by kinesiologists. Practiced in this country since 1964, it was originated by Dr. George Goodheart and his associates. Dr. John F. Thie advocates this method through the "Touch For Health" Foundation in Malibu, California. For more information and books available on the subject, interested readers can write to "Touch For Health" Foundation.

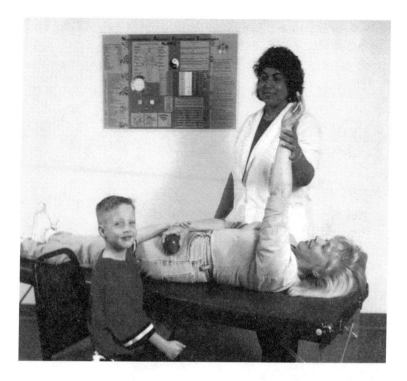

FIGURE 6-5
SURROGATE TESTING

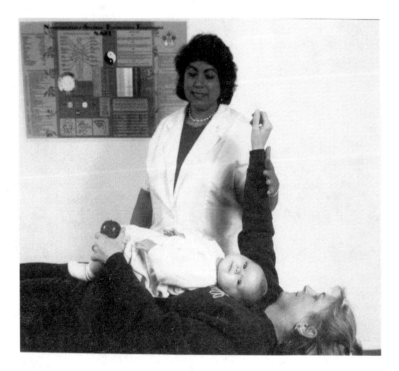

FIGURE 6-6
TESTING AN INFANT THROUGH A SURROGATE

Muscle response testing can be used to test any substance for allergies. Even human beings can be tested for each other in this manner. The subject lies down and touches the other person he or she wants tested. The tester pushes the arm of the subject as in steps 2 and 3. If the subject is allergic to the second person, the indicator muscle goes weak. If the subject is not allergic, the indicator muscle remains strong.

If people are allergic to each other, (between husband and wife, mother and child, father and son, patient and doctor, etc.) the allergy can affect a person in various ways. The husband and wife can be fighting all the time or their health can be affected. The same things can happen among other family members too. It is important to test the family members and other immediate associates for person to person allergy and if found, they should be treated for each other to obtain health, wealth and happiness.

Muscle response testing for allergies should be taught in every school and in every establishment. Everyone should learn to test to detect their allergies even if the treatment is not available. If you know your allergies, you can easily avoid them and that will help you somewhat.

Let's look at the history of 6-year-old Ray who suffered from severe allergies all his life. The second day of his life, he developed red angry looking rashes all over the body. He began spitting up every meal whether it was water or milk. He suffered from severe constipation, insomnia, irritability, colic pains and severe eczema. When he was 6 months old, his pediatrician suggested purse-string surgery (tightening up the lower segment of the esophagus to prevent continuous vomiting). His mother learned to test for allergies through MRT. Through MRT, she detected allergies to almost all his food except a couple of items. She fed him those non-allergic food items every day for four years, (cream of rice, non-fat carnation dry milk and water). He did fairly well on the special diet. His eczema was under control. He slept better. His constipation was relieved. His colic pain diminished. He appeared happy and friendly.

When he was four he began treatment through NAET. In a year or so, after being treated for various allergies, he was able to eat normal food and was ready for school. He is a healthy teenager now.

Just by knowing MRT and the testing procedure, Ray's mother could prevent unwanted surgeries on Ray. If we can teach testing skills to the mass media, allergic people can hope to become like Ray.

Medical professionals as well as the public should be educated to listen and look for various types of allergies when they cannot find the cause of a problem. Unless you are educated to know about the MRT testing, you do not know what to look for. As you have seen, the theory of energy blockages and diseases comes from oriental medicine. Oriental medicine also teaches that, if given a chance, with a little support, the body will heal itself.

CHAPTER SEVEN

BRAIN-BODY

CONNECTIONS

7

BRAIN-BODY-CONNECTIONS

The human body is made up of bones, flesh, nerves and blood vessels, which can only function in the presence of vital energy. Without this energy, the body is like an advanced efficient computer without an electrical power supply. Vital energy is not visible to the human eye, neither is electricity. No one knows how or why the vital energy gets into the body or how, when or where it goes when it leaves. However, it is true that without vital energy none of the body functions can take place. When the human body is alive vital energy flows freely through the energy pathways. The blood will be circulating through the blood vessels and distributing appropriate nutrients to various parts of the body.

The blood helps to exchange oxygen and carbon dioxide cleaning up the impurities of the body. When blood receives proper nutrients, the body and bones grow, and the flesh and nerves, in turn, can protect the body. All body parts will work as a unit, like an efficient factory with all functions working as designed. When vital energy stops flowing through the energy pathways, the human machine ceases to function and the person is pronounced dead.

The human body is the most efficient, well-organized, functional unit known. Many branches of channels and energy pathways connect each and every cell of the body (the basic building block) with every other cell. In turn, every body part is connected and interlinked by a meshing of networks of channels and branches, creating a perfect communication system within the body. The brain is the commander of this system. When the vital energy activates this system, the brain takes over the responsibilities. Under the brain's command, all parts of the body are activated; there is open communication between the brain, cells from different parts of tissue and other body parts. This communication takes place in a matter of nanoseconds; thus the brain maintains complete control of the body functions.

If for some reason a blockage takes place in the energy pathways, normal physiology is disrupted. This energy disruption will lead to certain visible effects in the human body and pathological symptoms will begin to appear. In the beginning, these pathological symptoms are seen around the blockage(s). Then they spread along the channels and branches to related tissues and organs. If the blockages affect the nerves that supply the different parts of the brain, diminished function of the brain is the result.

Traditional Chinese medicine describes the meridians as well as the symptoms of each of the primary channels. This chapter will explain the 12 primary channels and how blockages in these channels present physical and emotional symptoms, which cause illness, disease, and mental disorders. Many of the symptoms relating to blockages in the meridians will be familiar to the parents of children with ADHD. Only a brief overview is given in this chapter to aquaint you with energy meridians. You are encouraged to read or refer to any of the respective acupuncture textbooks named in the bibliography. Please read "Say Good-bye To Illness," by the author, for more extensive information about these meridians.

LUNG MERIDIAN

The inability of the lung meridian to accept fresh energy at 3:00 a.m. causes problems in the lung energy meridian. This blockage in the first meridian transmits into all other meridians as a chain reaction, and energy circulation gets disrupted.

LUNG MERIDIAN
PATHOLOGICAL SYMPTOMS

♦ Afternoon fever, acute bronchial asthmatic attacks, cardiac asthma, asthma worse after 3:00 a.m., shortness of breath, burning in the eyes and nostrils, chest congestion, cough, coughing up blood, dry mouth and throat, emaciated look, fever; itching of the nostrils, headaches between eyes, nasal congestion, nose bleed, postnasal drips, runny nose with clear discharge, red or painful eyes, sneezing, throat irritation, swollen throat, and swollen cervical glands.

♦ Excessive perspiration in some cases and lack of perspiration in others, husky voice, infection in the respiratory tract, influenza, irritability, low voice, lack of desire to talk, laryngitis, nasal polyps, night sweats, other chest infections, pleurisy, pneumonia, red cheeks, red eyes, pain in the eyes, sinus infections, and sinus headaches.

♦ Abdominal bloating, nausea, vomiting, constipation or loose stools, body ache, irritability, and restlessness.

♦ Chronic hives, cradle cap, eczema, excessive sweating, skin rashes, skin tags, moles, warts, scaly and rough skin, heat sensation with hot palms, hair loss, thinning of the hair, poor growth of hair and nails, rough ridges on the nails, and brittle nails.

Main Emotion: GRIEF

Related emotions: a tendency toward humiliating others, always apologizing, comparing self with others, contempt, dejection, depression (early morning), despair, emotionally super sensitive, expressions of over-sympathy, false pride, low self-esteem, hopelessness, insulting others, and intolerance.

Liking onion, peppers, garlic and cinnamon, pungent and spicy foods, and sometimes craving them.

Loneliness, meanness, melancholy, over demanding, prejudice, seeking others' approval, self-pity and weeping frequently without reason.

Nutrients Needed for Better Function:

Clear water, proteins, citrus fruits, cinnamon, onions, garlic, green peppers, black peppers, rice, vitamin C, bioflavonoids, and vitamin B-2.

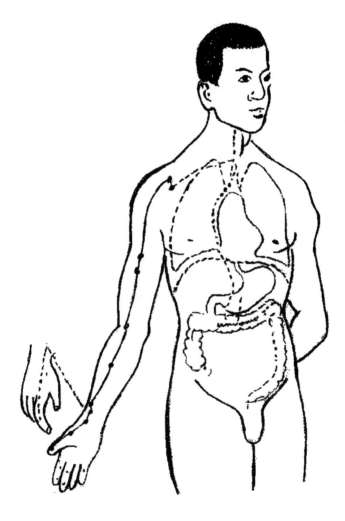

Figure 7-1
Lung Meridian

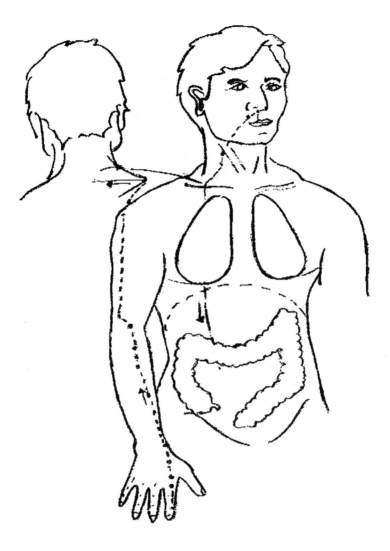

Figure 7-2
Large Intestine (LI)

LARGE INTESTINE MERIDIAN
PATHOLOGIC SYMPTOMS

♦   Dry mouth, throat, sore throat, nose bleed, toothache on lateral incisors, first lower and second lower bicuspid, red and painful eyes, swelling of the neck and swelling of the lateral part of the knee joint, pain in the shoulders, knees, parts of the thighs, and along the course of the meridan.

♦   Lower abdominal cramps, constipation or diarrhea, spastic colon, spasms of the rectum and anal sphincter, itching of the anus, generalized hives, intestinal noise, flatulence, bleeding from the rectum, colitis, and dizziness.

♦   Abdominal pain, bloating, bad breath, belching, chest congestion, shortness of breath and sinus headaches on the sides of the nose, between the eyes, and over the eyes.

♦   Acne, blister/inflammation of the lower gum, dermatitis, feeling better or tired after a bowel movement, hair loss, hair thinning, hives, and warts.

Main Emotion: GUILT

Related Emotions:

Grief, sadness, seeking sympathy, weeping, crying spells, and defensiveness.

Haunted by past painful memories, bad dreams, nightmares, talking in the sleep, rolling restlessly in sleep, and inability to recall dreams.

Nutrition Needed for better Function:

Vitamins A, D, E, C, B complex, especially B-1, wheat, bran, oat bran, yogurt, and roughage.

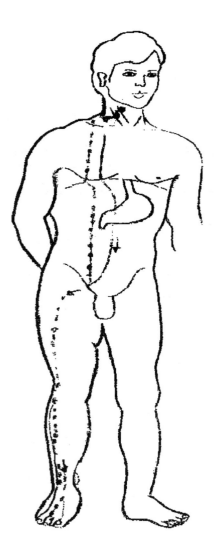

Figure 7-3
Stomach Meridian

STOMACH MERIDIAN
Pathologic Symptoms

This is one of the major meridians that is affected in ADD and ADHD patients.

♦ Frequent fever, sore throat, coated tongue, flushed face, fever blisters, herpes, sores on the gums and inside the lips, red painful boils on the face, sweating, cracks on the center of the tongue, bad breath, fatigue, insomnia, seizures, toothache, pain on the upper jaw and upper gum diseases, fibromyalgia and temporomandibular joint problems (TMJ).

♦ Pain in the eye and chest, pain along the course of the channel in the leg or foot, swelling on the neck, facial paralysis, and coldness in the lower limbs.

♦ Acne, heat boils or blemishes, black and blue discoloration along the channel, itching and red rashes along the lateral aspect of the lower leg below the knee.

♦ Abdominal bloating, fullness or edema, abdominal cramps, vomiting, nausea, anorexia, bulimia, hiatal hernia, and discomfort when reclining.

♦ Insomnia, restlessness, mental confusion, personality changes, double personality, hyperactivity in children or adults, manic-depressive behaviors, learning disorders, schizophrenia, lack of concentration, and aggressive behaviors.

♦ Obsession, obsessive compulsive behaviors, panic disorders, headaches on the forehead, and behind the eyes (dull, sharp, pressure or burning pain behind the eyes).

Main Emotion: DISGUST

Related emotions: bitterness, disappointment, greed, emptiness, deprivation, restlessness, obsession, egotism, and despair.
Lack of concentration, nostalgia, mental confusion, mental fog,
manic disorders, schizophrenia, hyperactivity, extreme nervousness, butterfly sensation in the stomach, and aggressive behaviors,
paranoia, fear of losing control, fear of dying, terror (a sense that
something unimaginably horrible is about to occur and one is pow-
erless to prevent it), and perceptual distortions.

Nutrition Needed for better Function:

B complex especially B-12, B-6, B-3 and folic acid.

SPLEEN MERIDIAN
Pathological Symptoms

This is one of the major meridians that is affected in ADD and ADHD patients.

Heaviness in the head, abdominal pain, fullness or distension, incomplete digestion of food, intestinal noises, nausea, vomiting, lack of taste, stiffness of the tongue, lack of smell, hard lumps in the abdomen, reduced appetite, craving sugar, indigestion, loose stools, diarrhea constipation, hypoglycemic reaction, general feverishness, and body aches.

Low self-esteem, procrastination, depression, and intuitive and prophetic behaviors. Pallor, tiredness, sleeplessness, sleepy in the afternoon, sleepy during the day, latent insomnia, dreams that makes you tired, dizzy spells, light-headedness, jaundice, fatigue, depression, weak limbs, anemia, bleeding disorders, and hemorrhoids.

Main Emotion: WORRY

Related emotion: over-concern, nervousness, keeps feelings inside, likes loneliness, hyperactivity in children or adults, manic depressive disorder, obsessive compulsive disorder, depression, panic attack, and does not like crowds.

Lack of self-confidence, gives more importance to self, hopelessness, irritable, likes to take revenge, likes to be praised, low self-esteem, unable to make decisions, shy, timid, restrained, easily hurt, talks to self, likes to get constant encouragement otherwise falls apart, likes to live through others, over-sympathetic to others.

Nutrition Needed For Better Function:

Vitamin A, vitamin C, calcium, chromium, and protein.

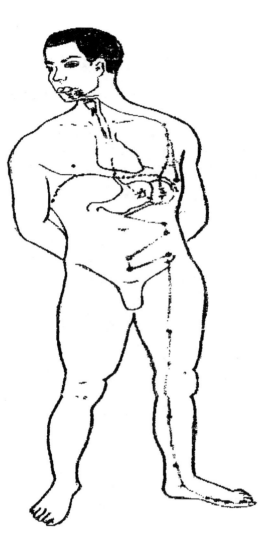

Figure 7-4
Spleen Meridian

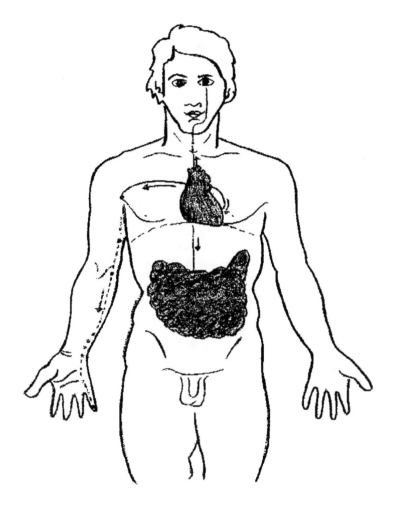

Figure 7-5

HEART MERIDIAN

HEART MERIDIAN
Pathological Symptoms

This is one of the meridians often seen imbalanced in people with ADHD.

♦ Poor circulation and dizziness, general feverishness, headache, and dry throat.

♦ Mental disorders, nervousness, hyperactivity in children or adults, bipolar disorder, manic depressive disorder, depression, panic attack, obsessive compulsive disorder, emotional excesses, sometimes abusive, and irritability.

♦ Vertigo, nausea, dizziness, or light-headedness.

♦ Shortness of breath, excessive perspiration, insomnia, chest distension, palpitation, heaviness in the chest and sharp chest pain, irregular heart beats, and chest distention.

Main Emotion: Joy

Over-excitement, emotional excess (excessive laughing or crying), sadness or lack of emotions.

Abusive nature, bad manners, anger, easily upset, aggressive personality, insecurity, hostility, guilt, does not make friends, and does not trust anyone.

Nutrition Needed for better Function
Calcium, vitamin C, vitamin E, and B complex.

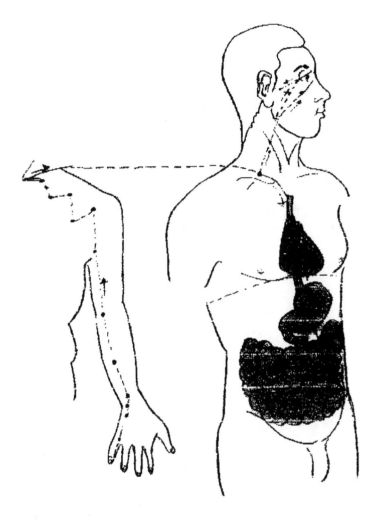

Figure 7-6
Small Intestine Meridian

SMALL INTESTINE MERIDIAN
Pathological Symptoms

♦ Distension and pain in the lower abdomen, pain radiating around the waist, and to the genitals.

♦ Abdominal pain with dry stool, constipation, and diarrhea. Knee pain, shoulder pain and frozen shoulder.

Main Emotion: INSECURITY

♦ Related emotion: emotional instability, feeling of abandonment, or desertion.

♦ Joy, over-excitement, sadness, sorrow, and suppression of deep sorrow.

♦ Absent-mindedness, poor concentration, daydreaming paranoia, and sighing.

♦ Irritability, easily annoyed, lacking the confidence to assert oneself, and shy.

♦ Becoming too involved with details, introverted, and easily hurt.

Nutrition Needed for better Function:

Vitamin B complex, vitamin D, vitamin E.
Acidophilus, yogurt, fibers, wheat germs, and whole grains.

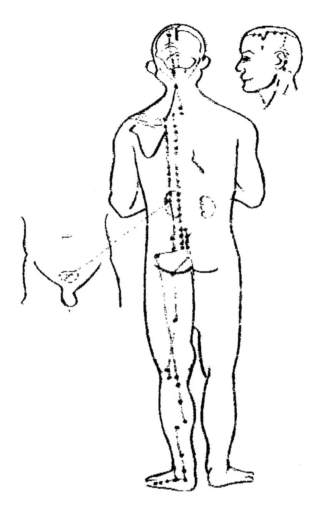

Figure 7-7
Bladder Meridian

BLADDER MERIDIAN
Pathological Ssymptoms

◆ Frequent, painful and burning urination, loss of bladder control and bloody urine.

◆ Chills, fever, headaches (especially at the back of the neck), stiff neck, nasal congestion, and disease of the eye.

◆ Pain: in the lower back, along back of the leg and foot, along the meridian, in the lateral part of the ankle, in the lateral part of the sole, in the little toe, and be hind the knee.

◆ Pain and discomfort in the lower abdomen, sciatic neu ralgia, spasm behind the knee, spasms of the calf muscles, weakness in the rectum and rectal muscle.

◆ Pain in the lower abdomen, enuresis, retention of urine, burning urination, bloody urine, painful urination, fre quent bladder infection, fever, and mental disorders.

◆ Chronic headaches at the back of the neck and pain at the inner canthus of the eyes.

Main Emotion: FRIGHT

Related emotions: holds on to sad, disturbing and impure thoughts, unable to let go of unwanted past memories, timid, inefficient, annoyed, highly irritable, fearful, unhappy, reluctant, restless, impatient, and frustrated.

Nutrition Needed For Better Function

Vitamin C, A, E, B complex, B-1, calcium, and trace minerals.

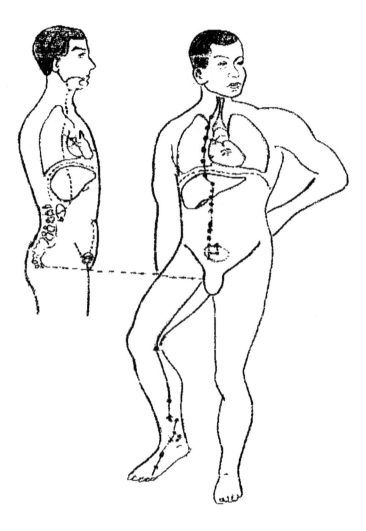

Figure 7-8
Kidney Meridian

KIDNEY MERIDIAN
Pathological Symptoms

♦ Pain: along the lower vertebrae, in the low back, and in the sole of the foot.
♦ Puffy eyes, bags under the eyes, and dark circles under the eyes.
♦ Motor impairment or muscular atrophy of the foot, dryness of the mouth, sore throat, pain in the sole of the foot, pain in the posterior aspect of the leg or thigh, and lower backache.
♦ Pain and ringing in the ears, light-headedness, and nausea.
♦ Frequent burning and painful urination.
♦ Fever, fever with chills, irritability, vertigo, facial edema, blurred vision, ringing in the ears, spasms of the ankle and feet, swelling in the legs, and swollen ankles.
♦ Loose stools, chronic diarrhea, constipation, abdominal distention, vomiting, tiredness, dry mouth, excessive thirst, poor appetite, and poor memory.

Main Emotion: FEAR

Related emotions: Indecision, terror, caution, confusion, seeks attention, unable to express feelings, lack of concentration, and poor memory.

Nutrition Needed for better Function
Vitamin A, E, B, essential fatty acids, calcium, and iron.

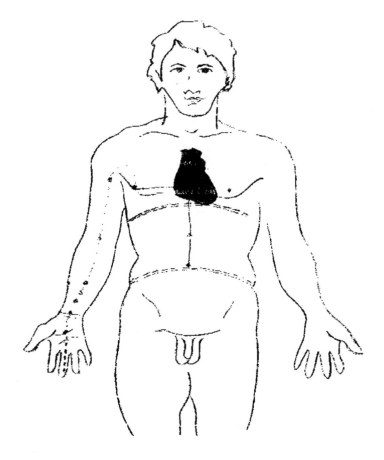

Figure 7-9
Pericardium Channel

PERICARDIUM MERIDIAN
Pathological Symptoms

♦ Stiff neck, spasms in the arm, spasms in the leg, spasms of the elbow and arm, frozen shoulder, restricting move ments, hot palms, and pain along the channels.

♦ Impaired speech, fainting spells, flushed face, irritability, fullness in the chest, heaviness in the chest, slurred speech.

♦ Sensation of hot or cold, nausea, nervousness, pain in the eyes, and sub-axillary swellings.

♦ Motor impairment of the tongue, palpitation, chest pain and heaviness in the chest due to emotional overload.

♦ Irritability, excessive appetite, fullness in the chest, and sugar imbalance.

Main Emotion: HURT and/or EXTREME JOY

Related emotions: over-excitement, regret, jealousy, sexual tension, stubbornness, manic disorders, heaviness in the head, light sleep with dreams, fear of heights, various phobias, imbalance in the sexual energy like never having enough sex or in some cases no sexual desire.

Nutrition Needed for better Function

Vitamin E, vitamin C, chromium, and trace minerals.

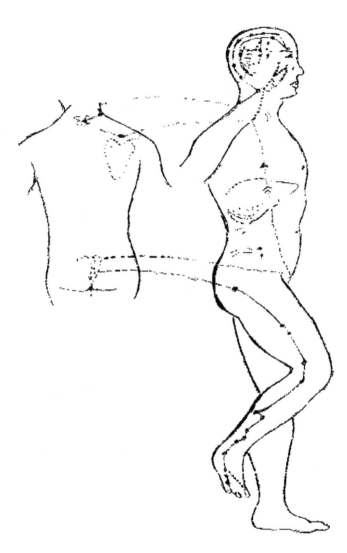

Figure 7-9
Triple Warmer Meridian

TRIPLE WARMER MERIDIAN
PATHOLOGICAL SYMPTOMS

♦ Swelling and pain in the throat, pain in the cheek and jaw, excessive hunger, redness in the eye, deafness, and pain behind the ear.

♦ Abdominal pain, distention, hardness and fullness in the lower abdomen, enuresis, frequent urination, and edema.

♦ Dysuria, excessive thirst, excessive hunger, always feels hungry even after eating, vertigo, indigestion, hypoglycemia, hyperglycemia, and constipation.

♦ Pain in the medial part of the knee, shoulder pain, and fever in the late evening.

Main Emotion: HOPELESSNESS

Related emotions: depression, despair, grief, excessive emotion, emptiness, deprivation, and phobias.

Nutrition Needed for better Function

Iodine, table salt, trace minerals, vitamin C, calcium, fluoride, and water.

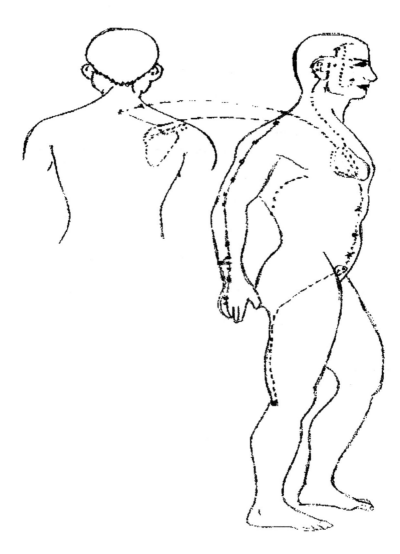

Figure 7-11
Gall Bladder Meridian

GALL BLADDER MERIDIAN
PATHOLOGICAL SYMPTOMS

♦ Alternating fever and chills, headache, ashen complexion, pain in the eye or jaw, swelling in subaxillary region, scrofula, and deafness.

♦ Pain: along the channel in the hip region, leg or foot and along the channel, tremors or twitching of the body or parts of the body.

♦ Vomiting and bitter taste in the mouth, ashen complexion, swelling in the sub-axillary region and deafness.

♦ A heavy sensation in the right upper part of the abdomen, sighing, dizziness, chills, fever, and yellowish complexion.

Main Emotion: RAGE

Related Emotions: assertion, aggression, shouting, and talking aloud.

Nutrition Needed for Better Function

Vitamin A, calcium, linoleic acids, and oleic acids (for example, pine nuts).

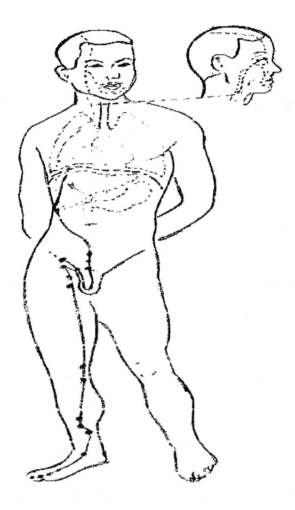

FIGURE 7-12
LIVER MERIDIAN

LIVER MERIDIAN
PATHOLOGICAL SYMPTOMS

This meridian is usually imbalanced in people with ADHD.

♦   Headache at the top of the head, vertigo, and blurred vision.

♦   Feeling of some obstruction in the throat, tinnitus, fever, spasms in the extremities and pain along the channel, abdominal pain, and hard lumps in the upper abdomen.

♦   Pain in the intercostal region, hernia, PMS, pain in the breasts, vomiting, jaundice, loose stools, and pain in the lower abdomen.

♦   Irregular menses, reproductive organ disturbances, and excessive bright colored bleeding during menses.

♦   Enuresis, retention of urine, dark urine, dizziness, and stroke-like condition.

Main Emotion: ANGER
Related emotions: aggression, hyperactivity, anger, frustration, unhappiness, complaining all the time, and finding faults with others.

Nutrition Needed for better Function
Beets, green vegetables, vitamin A, trace minerals, and unsaturated fatty acids.

CHAPTER EIGHT

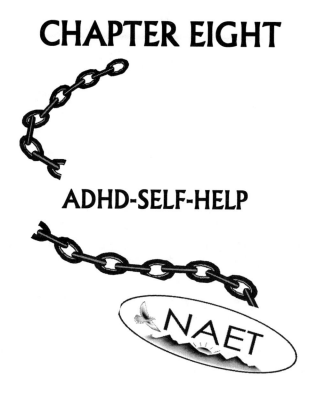

ADHD-SELF-HELP

8

ADHD SELF-HELP

Most of the acupuncture points used in eliminating the energy blockages lie near vital organs. The information about the treatment points and the techniques for needling the specific points to remove allergy are not described in this book. Each of these points is needled with special techniques, which are taught in acupuncture colleges. Teaching these techniques is beyond the scope of this book and has been intentionally excluded. Needling in these areas requires proper education and extensive practice. Improper needling can cause damage to vital organs and even greater damage to health, sometimes leading to fatal accidents.

There are thousands of doctors trained in NEAT treatment methods all over the country. Please visit our website "naet.com" to find a practitioner near you.

Information regarding a few important acupuncture points is discussed in this chapter. They can be used to help control ADD or ADHD at any age. It is not a cure. It is going to provide temporary relief from the symptoms.

In Chapter Seven we learned about the twelve acupuncture meridians and their pathological symptoms when the energy circulation is blocked in those meridians (diagrams 7-1 to 7-12). In Chapter 6, "Muscle-Response Testing," we learned to detect the cause of energy blockages by testing via MRT for allergies. We also found that allergies may be the causative agents for energy blockages in particular meridians. We have learned to test and find the causes in general. Practice these testing techniques and make a habit of testing your child for everything before exposing yourself, your child or your loved one's to food, clothing, household chemicals, and environmental agents, etc., which you know or suspect are allergens.

Table 8-1 / POINTS TO BALANCE THE ORGANS

Point Name	Related Meridian	Related Organ
Pt 0	Brain Test Pt	Brain
Pt 1	LU test pt	Lung
Pt 2	PHT(physical heart)	Pericardium
Pt 3	LIV test pt	Liver
Pt 4	GB test pt	Gall bladder
Pt 5	Heart test pt	Heart
Pt 6	ST test pt	Stomach
Pt 7	Kid test pt	Kidney
Pt 8	Sp test pt	Speen
Pt 9	Colon test pt	Colon
Pt 10	TW test pt	Triple warmer
Pt 11	SI test pt	Small Intestine
Pt 12	BI test pt	Bladder

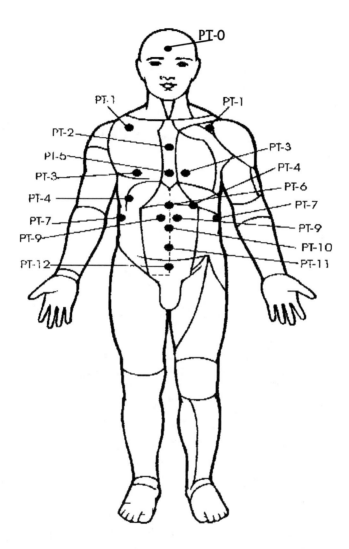

Figure 8-1
Points to Balance the Organs

ISOLATING THE BLOCKAGES

Testing and isolating the particular blockages can be done in many ways. One method, described here, is fairly easy to understand and with some practice this art can be mastered by anyone.

STEP 1. Balance the patient and find an indicator muscle. Refer to Chapter 7 to learn more about NTT and MRT to test your allergies.

STEP 2. The patient lies down on his back with the allergen (e.g., an apple) in his resting palm. When it is needed, surrogate testing can also be used.

STEP 3. The tester touches the point in diagram 8-1 one at a time, and tests the pre-determined muscle and compares the strength of the PDM in the absence and presence of the allergen. For example, touch point '1' in diagram 8-1 with the finger tips of one hand and with the other hand test the indicator muscle, (while the patient is still holding the allergen in one hand). The muscle goes weak, indicating that the meridian or the energy pathways connected to that particular point has an energy blockage.

Point '1' relates to the lung meridian. Obstruction in the energy flow anywhere in the lung meridian can make this point weak. Test the PDM, while touching each point in the lung meridian (for more information regarding point location in the meridians please refer to the appropriate books on acupuncture given in the bibliography). The indicator muscle becomes weakest when the tester touches sites of the blocked area in the meridian. For point-meridian relationships, refer to table 8-1. Using this technique, you can trace all weak meridians and the specific weak sites in your body.

Finger pressure therapy can be used temporarily to restore the energy flow in the blocked energy meridians.

STEP 1. The first step for finger pressure therapy is to find the organ or meridian being blocked. Find the related organ point on the table and then in the diagram 8-1.

STEP 2. Apply slight finger pressure, with the pad of your index finger, on the point. Hold 60 seconds at each point. Follow the order of the sequence of points given on the previous page. When the blocked meridian is found, make the associated organ point with that meridian a starting point to perform the energy balancing. For example, if the energy is blocked in the liver meridian, make the liver organ point (point 3) the first point to begin the finger pressure. If the heart is blocked, use the heart point (point 5) as the first point in the sequence of energy balancing.

STEP 3. Hold 60 seconds at each point and go through all 12 points and come back to the starting point. Then, hold 60 seconds at the starting point and stop the treatment. Always end at the starting point to complete the energy cycle.

Some patients can experience physical or emotional pain or emotional release during these treatment sessions. If the patient has an emotional blockage, it needs to be isolated and treated for the best result. Some patients can get tingling pains, sharp pains, pulsation, excessive perspiration, etc. during the treatment. In such instances, please go through another cycle of treatment. Often this will correct the problem.

Some commonly used acupuncture points, and their uses to help in emergency situations, are given below. Massage these points gently with the finger pads for one minute each. Please refer to the appropriate meridians in Chapter 7 or refer to the textbooks on acupuncture in the bibliography if you would like to learn more about these points.

RESUSCITATION POINTS

1. Fainting: GV 26, GB 12, LI 1, PC 9
2. Nausea: CV 12, PC 6
3. Backache: GV 26, UB 40
4. Fatigue: CV 5, LI 1, CV 17
5. Fever: LI 11, LU 10, GV 16

For more information on revival techniques, refer to Chapter 3, pages 570 to 573, in "Acupuncture: A Comprehensive Text", by Shanghai College of Traditional Medicine, Eastland Press, 1981 or refer to "Living Pain Free with Acupressure" by the author. It is available at various bookstores and at our website (naet.com).

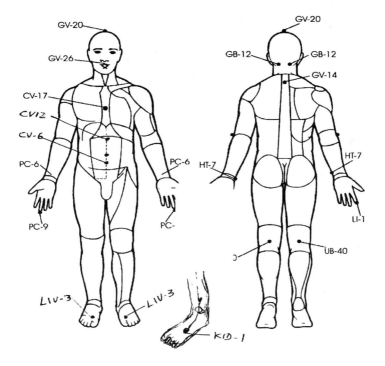

Figure 8-2
RESUSCITATION POINTS

Allergy treatments require repeated office visits in the beginning. Once all the known allergens are eliminated, the patient is trained to find his/her own allergens. The patient then has to see the doctor only if he/she encounters an item that bothers him/her and cannot be eliminated using the above methods, or for annual follow-ups. All allergens cannot be eliminated in one or two office visits. In some severe cases, it may take as many as three visits a week for one to two years or more to achieve a condition close to normalcy. This is contingent on the patient's immune system response.

There have been a few patients with mild cases of allergies who have completed the treatments in one or two visits or in two or three months. These patients were either not seen again, or only on a few follow-up visits. On the average, most patients have taken anywhere from eight to twelve months to achieve satisfactory results. Some extreme cases have taken three-and-half to four years to solve their problems. Allergic patients should keep this time span in mind when they approach any NAET specialists. If treatment is discontinued before completion of all the necessary treatments, the results will be unsatisfactory and allergic symptoms are very likely to recur. This will tend to make the patient feel that the allergy itself is to blame or that the treatment is useless. For this reason, it is better not even to start treatment, than to start and discontinue too soon or, to start and then cooperate in a half-hearted manner. The allergist will discharge his patients with proper instructions, just as soon as he/she feels it is safe to do so.

How can patients cooperate and help the doctor achieve maximum results in minimum time? After each treatment, patients are advised to stay away from the treated item for 24 hours. There are 12 energy meridians. In order for an energy molecule to pass through one meridian it takes two hours. To circulate through 12 meridians, it takes 24 hours. This means that the patient should not even come close to the object, as its electromagnetic field can interfere with the patient's own field and negate the treatment. Patients are also advised to maintain a food diary. Thus, if the patient reacts to something violently during treatment, the offender can easily be traced and treated, preventing further pain. During treatment, patients are placed on a strict diet of non-allergic items after the completion of three treatments. This helps the body to maintain good health without having to face possible allergic items. It also speeds up the treatment process while reducing interference.

The following is a list of general directions which, it is hoped, will be of assistance to allergic patients, regardless of the particular symptoms they may suffer. ·

1. The best time to begin treatments for your symptoms is now. Do not wait until it gets severe. It is not likely that the symptoms will decrease with the passing of time without doing anything; more likely, the symptoms will become more severe.

2. Report regularly for treatment and as often as directed by your NAET specialist. If necessary, long breaks should only be taken after completion of the treatment for each item. Never take more than two days off without completing a treatment for each item. For example, when getting treated for a milk allergy if you were to take five consecutive visits to clear the allergy to milk, you should take a few days or a week off after passing the treatment only. After being cleared of the milk, and before starting treatment for another item like beef, you may take a break.

3. Certain people may have a negative reaction to a treatment. One cannot predict reactions ahead of time. For this reason, the patient has to remain in the doctor's office anywhere from 15 minutes to half-an-hour following the treatment. During that time, if there is an unusual reaction, the doctor will treat the patient again.

If there is no reaction, the patient will be sent home with certain instructions to follow.

4. The patient should not come close to the energy field of the items after he/she leaves the doctor's office for a period of 25 hours. This is a crucial time because the brain works on a biological time clock of 24-hour cycles. You should leave one hour extra for the brain to adjust. During this time, the brain can reject or accept the treatment. If the brain accepts the treatment, it will generally not reject it for the rest of the patient's life.

5. Soon after treatment, patients should avoid strenuous activity, exercises, heavy meals, etc., for at least three to four hours. It is possible that any of these activities can cause a sudden blockage in the energy pathway causing unpleasant reactions.

6. Patients, who are allergic to many items, will experience various symptoms if they use the allergenic items while they are undergoing treatment. In NAET treatment, the patient is asked to use or eat anything he wants except for the item for which he/she is getting treated. If he/she is eating some other allergen, he/she can still react to that particular allergen even though this does not interfere with the current treatment; however, the patient may not feel very good. For better and faster results, the patient should avoid all other allergens. If the patient is under any other medical care for any other symptoms, he/she is advised to continue those other treatments as before, along with the NAET treatments. This will help the patient keep his/her other health problems under control while going through the allergy treatments. This way the body does not have to fight stress or diseases from different causes while undergoing the stress of the new treatment. Patients who have ADD, ADHD should continue their medicines or other treatments, so that they can get through these allergy treatments more easily

than patients who refuse to seek western medical supportive treatments and rely on the allergy treatments alone.

7. During treatment, patients are advised to avoid exposure to extreme weather, such as excessive heat and cold drafts.

8. Patients are advised to practice good nutrition. They should try to eat non-allergenic items, or items that have been treated, while going through this program. Patients are also advised not to overeat or over-exercise, to drink plenty of liquids, have pleasant thoughts while preparing and eating the foods, and get plenty of rest.

9. Remember that it usually takes several years to build up sensitivity to the point where severe reactions occur. Do not get discouraged if relief from symptoms is delayed for some time. Just because all the symptoms do not disappear at the end of a few days or weeks of treatment, there is no reason for discontinuing a diet or the treatments. When a few major allergies are cleared, minor allergies may be noticed more easily. Your awareness of allergies will be more pronounced after a few items have been cleared. Some patients ask, "After being cleared for some items, do I become more allergic to things I was not allergic to before?" The answer is a definite "No." the person's awareness increases, or the allergic reactions stick out more noticeably after some major items have been cleared.

10. Avoid emotional stress and undue worry. This will bring down the immune system by increasing the energy blockages and cause more allergic reactions. If you are under a lot of stress, or sadness, you should avoid heavy meals, excessively spicy or salty meals. Try to eat simple foods in liquid or pureed form to allow the food to go through the digestive tract faster without dispensing a lot of energy from the energy reservoir.

11. As you improve, your symptoms will grow less severe and less frequent, but do not stop the treatments. Try to complete treatments for all your known allergies. Otherwise, untreated allergens may build up and cause problems later.

12. Severely allergic patients should always try to carry antihistamines and oral medications or adrenaline shots with them. Severely allergic patients can get into life-threatening situations at any time with any kind of allergy. If the patient can administer the adrenaline shot or antihistamines immediately, the after-effect will be less severe preventing unfortunate incidents.

Additionally, specific instructions will be necessary for each patient, and these instructions vary depending on his/her sensitivities and allergic manifestations.

CHAPTER NINE

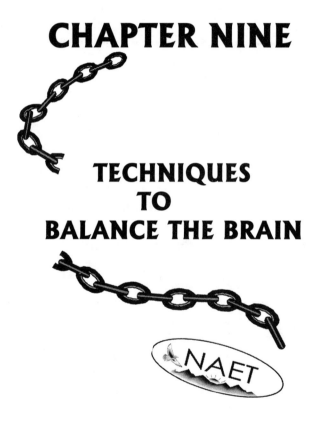

TECHNIQUES
TO
BALANCE THE BRAIN

NAET

9

TECHNIQUES TO BALANCE THE BRAIN

Most of the cases of attention deficit hyperactive disorders I have seen fall into the category of allergy-based ADHD due to two factors:

1. My patients come from referrals; so allergic patients may be referring other patients with allergic symptoms to my office. Symptoms of ADD and ADHD overlap allergic symptoms.

2. Allergy may be the major cause of ADHD.

Allergy causes brain imbalance, as we have seen in the previous chapters. Brain imbalances arising from allergies are probably due to an improper response of the immune system affecting the brain or certain parts of the brain by otherwise harmless substances. An allergic person can react to anything around him, creating various health problems, which involve every part and organ of the body or impair any function of the body. So the brain and its associated organs are not any different from other vital organs in the body.

Ever since the appearance of Ritalin, or similar stimulants, many families have benefited from this drug to help calm their children, perform well in school, behave appropriately in social situations, and cooperate better at home.

During the past decade many controversies and concerns have been raised about the use of this medication. Some studies reported an increase in substance abuse among the users of this type of stimulant, while other research revealed a history of stunted growth among the regular users.

A survey done by Los Angeles Times in August 1999, reported that children with attention deficit hyperactive disorder (no matter what kind of treatment they receive) are more likely to abuse drugs---including tobacco, alcohol, marijuana, cocaine and stimulants---than children without ADHD.

"If the medication has a good effect, which it does in 80% of children, then it reduces a lot of stress and anxiety. And that would be the mechanism to reduce substance abuse. But it doesn't do it in all cases," says Dr. James Swanson, a UCI (University of California, Irvine) professor of Pediatrics and a leading researcher on ADHD.

But according to Mathew Cohen, president of the children with Attention Deficit Disorders, a national support group based in Landover, MD., we hear different version. He strongly believes that children who do not receive help in coping with the problems related to ADHD may wind up as social outcasts or school dropouts, which in turn can lead to substance abuse.

However, Nadine Lambert, a UC Berkeley education professor, who is an expert in learning disorders, suggests that animal studies show that users of stimulants can become sensitized to the drug.

While western medicine attempts short-term chemotherapeutic cures for ADD and ADHD, as with Ritalin, we have achieved a longer-lasting, more effective, non-drug, non-invasive modality: N.A.E.T.

We now know that most of the causes of common illnesses including ADD and ADHD are in fact, undiagnosed allergies when left untreated, can become serious health problems. An allergy is an over-reaction of the immune system. In NAET, allergies are viewed from a holistic perspective based on oriental medical principles.

When the body, or a magnetic field of the body, makes contact with an allergen, it causes blockages in the energy pathways called meridians. In another way, we can say, it disrupts the normal flow of energy through the body's electrical circuits. This energy blockage causes interference in communication between the brain and body via the nervous system. The obstructed energy flow is the first step in a chain of events, which can develop into an allergic response. An allergic reaction is the result of continuous energy imbalances in the body, leading to a diminished state of health in one or more organs.

The energy pathways traveling back and forth from brain to the heart, spleen, and liver meridians are affected in ADHD cases. NAET uses NTT to test the allergens and to detect blockages in meridians - Read Chapter three).

A DIAGNOSTIC EVALUATION OF ADHD BY NAET SHOULD INCLUDE:

• A thorough medical and family history; pre-natal history of the mother (if she suffered from any potentially related condition or emotional trauma during pregnancy, etc.); emotional, social and environmental history (parental divorce, child abuse, death of a loved one, environmental or residential disruption, a newcomer in the family or arrival of a new sibling).

• Behavior ratings completed by parents and teacher.

• A physical examination (vital signs, growth pattern, etc.).

• List of commonly eaten foods and drinks, any special addictions to toys, blankets,and furniture, etc. (could be allergic to any one of them).

• Muscle Response Testing for possible allergens.

• A computerized non-invasive testing for possible allergens.

• EEG reading of the brain if possible.

• Blood serum study either by ELIZA or ALCAT test

WESTERN APPROACHES
Western medical approaches for such conditions are:

• Behavior modification
• Educational modification
• Psychological counseling
• Pharmaceutical drugs

Medication has proven temporarily effective but does not provide long-term cure for many children with ADHD. In most cases, central nervous system stimulants are used. They are believed to stimulate the action of the brain's neurotransmitters, which enables the brain to regulate attention, impulse and behavior. Short acting stimulants like Dexedrine or Ritalin (methylphenidate) are commonly used. Ritalin has been used in the treatment of ADHD for several decades. It has been found helpful in alleviating the symptoms in children and adults who take the medication. In some cases where stimulants are not effective, antidepressants are used. Antidepressants can help to reduce or control many of the symptoms the child exhibits while the child continues learning and working. If there are no side effects, it is permissible to use medication to help the child function. It is certainly better than letting the child waste his/her life away. But it is very important to check for an allergy to the medication before administering it. If the child is allergic to the drug, it is not going to give the expected results. In some children an allergy to drugs could make their condition worse. They may become hyper, violent, irritable beyond control, and may display unpleasant side effects like itching, hives, eczema, indigestion, bowel and bladder incontinence, etc. In such cases, medication must be stopped immediately and should not be used again until the allergy is removed.

ADHD children are allergic to many foods and chemicals they use in their daily lives. Some children may outgrow these allergic symptoms and lead normal lives in their adulthood without the use of drugs or NAET. Others may need to continue the use of drugs and increase the dosage steadily to get the desired effect. They may have to continue the drug into adulthood, middle age and old age, if they did not eliminate their allergies.

One of the problems with using medication is that it is often given too quickly, before investigating other ways to help children with ADHD. Certain schools make it mandatory that parents give

Ritalin in order for the ADD child to continue attending school. Doctors readily prescribe this "magic pill" and for some children, it seems to work. This is easier than altering the lifestyle by behavior modification, changing the diet, and tracking down the actual cause of the problem for each individual child.

Even though western medical practitioners are using thoroughly researched pharmaceutical drugs, they are chemical compounds, which can have related allergy and side effects in certain individuals. The allergic reactions and side effects have created constant fear in some people discouraging them from using drugs. More and more people are becoming negative about taking drugs and are using products made by natural means. Long term use of chemicals can destroy our body's garbage disposal – the Liver— sometimes damage is irreversible!

ALTERNATIVE THERAPIES

Practitioners and consumers are looking for natural means to control this disorder. Out of necessity, many alternative therapies have been developed. There are many alternative therapies available for ADHD today that produce inner calmness and serenity in the victims without using drugs. These commonly practiced alternative therapies include:

• Behavior modification in conjunction with vitamin-mineral therapy.
• Amino-acid therapy.
• Various detoxification programs to remove toxins and parasites.
• Herbal supplementation, biofeedback, and a chemical-free environment.

- Diet management (removing sugar, corn, gluten, milk, dairy products, yeast, food additives, and carbonated water from the diet entirely).
- Providing regular chiropractic and acupuncture treatments.
- Regular therapeutic massages, saunas.
- Encouraging Yoga and meditation practices.
- Magnetic therapy.
- Engaging in regular sports and exercises programs.
- NAET

Now we have NAET, which has proven to be the most effective allergy treatment available so far.

NAET TREATMENT FOR ADHD

THE THREE STEP NAET TREATMENT:

STEP - 1

Isolate the offending allergen using NTT (Nambudripad's Testing Techniques - Chapter three) comparing the strength of a particular muscle in the body in the presence and absence of a suspected allergen. It is also called Muscle Response Testing, slightly different from MRT as in applied kinesioly. A computerized skin resistance test is used with allergens and the use of standardized laboratory tests RAST, ELIZA (enzyme-linked immunozorbant assay), etc., is encouraged.

STEP-2

Mild acupressure on specific pre-determined acupuncture points by the practitioner on the specific meridians.

STEP-3

Complete avoidance of the treated allergen for 25 hours following the treatment or otherwise determined by the practitioner. After 25 hours, the practitioner needs to retest the treated allergen to determine the completeness of the treatment. In most cases, it takes one treatment per single group of allergen (one office visit) to eliminate the allergy, if the treatment is administered properly and the 25-hour avoidance period is properly followed. In some extreme cases, it may take more than one office visit per group of items.

Avoiding the allergens is not always easy. In fact, it can be very cumbersome. The most effective treatment option for allergies until now has been complete avoidance of the offending allergens, which can be difficult and in some cases, impossible.

Can you imagine being on a diet month after month and year after year, especially if that diet contains no egg, soy, fruits, vegetables, wheat, corn, rice, sugar, fats, hamburgers, French fries, ice cream, milk, butter, oils, gluten, MSG, spices, whitenall, food additives, and food colorings, etc.? That's where NAET comes in. NAET will accommodate our "21st century lifestyles." It doesn't mean that you should go out of your way to eat any junk food available after completing NAET treatments.

NAET can remove the adverse effect of any allergic food in the body and create homeostasis in the presence of the offending allergen (without avoiding it for life). During the NAET treatment, your brain will create a new friendly memory for the allergen and will imprint and store this new memory in your memory bank. During this process, the old memory of the allergen's adverse effect is erased or forgotten. After completion of the NAET treatment, the allergen becomes a non-allergen, and an irritant becomes a non-irritant to your energy field. The body will learn to relax naturally in the presence of the new friendly substance. When the brain is not frightened about contact with the new harmless substance (previously an allergen), natural calmness comforts the brain and body. Thus the attention deficit and hyperactive symptoms will disappear. The child can relax and listen to others once again, without being bothered by the irritation that the allergen once produced. Now the calm nervous system will cooperate with the child and allow him/her to relax without the help of CNS stimulant or depressant. After treatment, if the child continues to maintain an allergy-free body and live in a suitable environment, he/she can say good-bye to ADHD forever.

SUPPORTIVE TREATMENTS WITH NAET

1 Brain Nectar
2 Brain Release
3 Acupoint Balance
4 Cross Crawl
5 Gait Training
6 Meridian balancing
7 Organ Balancing
8 Posture balance – standing
9 Posture Balance – sitting
10 Herbal Remedy

One or more of these techniques can be used to improve the stability of a child or an adult suffering from ADD or ADHD

1. BRAIN NECTAR

Make sure the ADD person is allergy-free to the following ingredients before you prepare the nectar.

If you find an allergy to one or two items, please exclude them from the drink until you clear the allergy to them. Each one of the ingredients enter the 12 meridians and helps to flush toxins out of the associated organ by strengthening the respective organ and channel.

1 pinch of dry lemon peel powder (Lung)
1 pinch of cayenne pepper powder (Ht)
1 pinch of dry ginger powder (St)
1 teaspoon barley green powder (Sp)
6 ounces of apple juice (Liver)
¼ teaspoon of flax seed powder (GB)
1/8 teaspoon of soybean powder (Kidney)
1 pinch of saffron powder (PC)
1 pinch of cinnamon (TW)
¼ teaspoon of clarified butter (Brain & nervous system)
¼ teaspoon of grape seed oil (LI)
1 ounce of pomegranate juice (SI)
1 tablespoonful of honey (Brain & nervous system)
50 mgs B complex vitamin (Brain & nervous system)
1 pinch of epsom salt (Brain & nervous system)
1 pinch of dry coriander powder (Brain & nervous system).

Blend all the ingredients in apple juice and drink four ounces twice a day on an empty stomach or one-two hours before meals. Also try to drink four-six glasses of purified water daily.

3. BRAIN RELEASE

The child lies on his/her back. The mother/helper sits next to his/her head, supporting the head in her left palm as in diagram 9-1. Find the point just above the eyebrows on the forehead and with the left palm lightly massage up to the top of the head while the child breathes in. When you get to the top of the head, gently release the hand and the child breathes out. Do this sweeping massage three times. Turn the head to one side. Support the head with one palm on the side cupping the ear with the supporting palm. Massage gently up the side of the cheek, in front of the opposite ear, while the child breathes in. The child breathes out as you reach the top of the head. Do both sides this way. Support the head with both hands and apply gentle traction towards you while encouraging the child to breathe in and out. Finally, massage the vertex or the top of the head for 30 seconds. This massage helps to get rid of the toxins from the brain.

2. ACU-POINT MASSAGE:

The right way to begin the day for an ADD child is shown in the diagram 9-2. Simply apply gentle finger pressure on the points in the order given in the diagram. Fifteen seconds on each point twice a day, in the morning when waking up and before going to sleep. Begin from the right hand, then go to the left hand, left leg, right leg and end up at the beginning point on the right hand. The points are numbered accordingly for easy understanding.

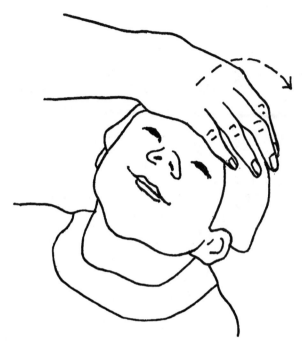

**FIGURE 9-1
BRAIN RELEASE**

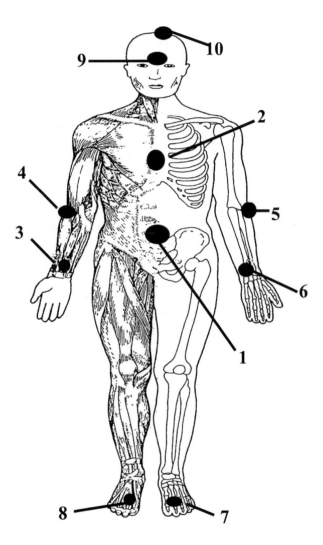

Figure 9-2
Acupoint Massage

4. CROSS-CRAWL

Usually the balance between the left and right halves of the brain is altered in an ADHD child or adult. This is known as switching. There are several reasons why one gets unbalanced or switched. Some of the common causes are anxiety, fear, lack of liquids in the body and allergies. Hydrating the patient alone helps to balance the two hemispheres most of the time. The kinesiological exercise "cross-crawl" as given in diagram 9-3 has been used for decades by kinesiologists to balance the left and right brain very effectively.

METHODOLOGY

The child lies down in a supine position (on his back). Make the child lift his/her right hand 90 degrees to the body and the left leg 45-90 degrees to the body. Hold for 10 seconds, then relax. The child then lifts his/her left-hand 90 degrees to the body and right leg 45-90 degrees to the body. Hold for 10 seconds, then relax. This completes one cycle. Repeat this cycle five times in the morning and five times in the evening.

5. GAIT TRAINING

ADHD children tend to walk with one arm swinging and other arm kept still. Make the child walk with both arms swinging as in diagram 9-4. Right foot forward, left hand forward; left foot forward, right hand forward just like a cross crawl. Do not let the child carry anything in his/her hands while walking because it will prevent swinging both arms. Gait Training also helps to balance the right and left brain. This gait has great therapeutic value not only to the brain, but also to the entire body. For further informa-

Figure 9-3
Cross crawl

Figure 9-4
Gait Training

tion, refer to the book "BEHAVIORAL KINESIOLOGY" by John Diamond, M.D.

6. MERIDIAN BALANCING

Have a set of meridian therapy cards, a energy chart or look at the travel pathways of twelve acupuncture meridians in Chapter Seven of this book or Chapter 10 in "Say Good-bye to Illness" by me. (meridian therapy cards and meridian charts are available from the NAET website store: www.naet.com). Gently trace the meridians bilateral on your body from the beginning of the first meridian of the energy cycle (Lung meridian) to the last one (Liver meridian). Run your fingers over the meridians with a gentle caressing action toward their flow (marked with 'start' and 'end' in the beginning and end of the meridians and an arrow denoting the flow along the black long lines on the meridian therapy cards). Follow the order of the meridians as given in Chapter Seven. Do once a day, preferably at bedtime. This helps to calm all the nerves in the body by removing the energy blockages from the energy pathways by gentle massage towards the flow of meridians.

7. ORGAN BALANCING

Begin at the first organ and work your way to the last one. Follow the order given in the diagram 9-5.

Method: Place your left palm face down on the first organ, right palm on the second organ. Leave them there for few seconds (10-15 seconds), until you feel the pulsation under your palm. Then move your left palm to the third organ, right palm to the fourth organ. Always move the left palm first, then right palm to create a continuity of the energy movement. Do not move both hands together; it breaks the energy cycle. When you reach the 12th organ

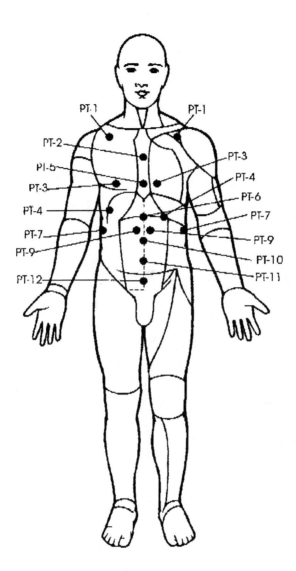

Figure 9-5
Organ Balancing

Figure 9-6
Postural Balancing-Standing

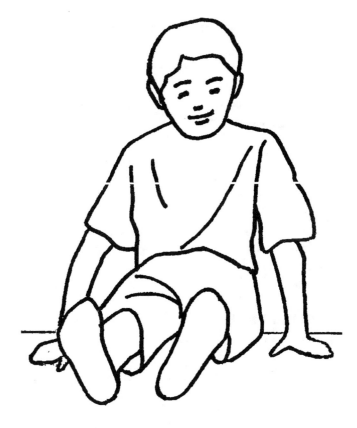

Figure 9-7
Postural Balancing – Sitting

point move your left hand back on the right lung for 15 seconds, then stop. Do once a day, preferably at bedtime.

8. POSTURAL BALANCING – STANDING

Make the child stand against a board, a smooth wall, or a door, etc. as in the diagram 9-6. The back of the head, both shoulders, the whole back, back of the knees, and the heels should be touching the wall or a flat surface. Make the child take a couple of deep breaths, then ask him to relax. Repeat this five times daily.

9. POSTURAL BALANCING – SITTING

Make the child sit against a board, a smooth wall, or a door, etc. The back of the head, both shoulders, the whole back, should be touching the wall or a flat surface. The back of the knees and the heels should be resting flat on the floor with the legs extended as in the diagram, figure 9-7. Make the child take couple of deep breaths, then ask him to relax. Repeat this five times. Do it once a day. This helps to teach the child discipline.

10. HERBAL REMEDY

Minor Cinnamon and Peony formula 1/2 gram x 3 with a glass of warm water 30 minutes after meals for children between the ages 3- 10 years. For older children and adults adjust the dosage to 2 grams daily or follow the suggested dosage on the bottle. This herbal remedy is very effective to remove brain irritability and restore calmness. Find out the correct dosage and the length of supplementation for the individual child or adult using the method "How to test and adjust the dosage of vitamins herbs, and medication" described in the NAET Guidebook. Always test for allergies before using it. The herbal remedy is available at:

Lotus Herbs,
1124 N. Hacienda Blvd.
La Puente, CA 91626
(626) 916-1070

CHAPTER TEN

ADHD

AND

ALLERGENS

10

ADHD AND ALLERGENS

Children and adults suffering from the symptoms of ADD and ADHD are usually allergic to the following food groups, which are listed according to their importance for the body. It is necessary to follow the restricted diet and your NAET specialist's instructions carefully during the 25 hours after the treatment in order to clear for the allergen being treated. You may also refer to the NAET Guidebook for more information on NAET treatments and specific instructions to follow during the 25 hour-avoidance period.

Most ADD and ADHD children and adults can get their symptoms under control when they complete NAET BASIC 15 groups of allergens successfully. Some ADHD children and adults with mild to moderate symptoms would show marked improvements after they complete just five basic groups of allergens. But it is for their advantage to complete the 35-40 groups of allergens before they stop the treatments.

1.**Egg Mix** (egg white, egg yolk, chicken, and tetracycline).
You may only eat brown or white rice, pasta without eggs, vegetables, fruits, milk products, oils, beef, pork, fish, coffee, juice, soft drinks, water, and tea.

2. **Milk and Calcium** (breast milk, cow's milk, goat's milk, and calcium).
You may only eat cooked rice, cooked fruits and vegetables (like potato, squash, green beans, yams, cauliflower, sweet potato), chicken, red meat, and drink coffee, tea without milk, or calicum-free water.

3. **Vitamin C** (fruits, vegetables, vinegar, citrus, and berry).
You may only eat cooked white or brown rice, pasta without sauce, boiled or poached eggs, baked or broiled chicken, fish, red meat, brown toast, deep fried food, French fries, salt, oils, and drink coffee or water.

4. **B complex vitamins (17 B-vitamins).**
You may only eat cooked white rice, cauliflower raw or cooked, well cooked or deep fried fish, salt, white sugar, black coffee, French fries, and purified, non allergic water when treating for any of the B vitamins. Rice should be washed well before cooking. It should be cooked in lots of water and drained well to remove the fortified vitamins.

5. **Sugar Mix** (cane sugar, corn sugar, maple sugar, grape sugar, rice sugar, brown sugar, beet sugar, fructose, molasses, honey, dextrose, glucose, and maltose).
You may only eat white rice, pasta, vegetables, vegetable oils, meats, eggs, chicken, water, coffee, tea without milk.

6. **Iron Mix** (animal and vegetable sources, beef, pork, lamb, raisin, date, and broccoli).
You may only eat white rice without iron fortification, sour dough bread without iron, cauliflower, white potato, chicken light green vegetables (white cabbage, iceberg lettuce, white squash, yellow squash, and orange juice).

7. **Vitamin A** (animal and vegetable source, beta carotene, fish and shell fish).
You may eat only cooked rice, pasta, potato, cauliflower, red apples, chicken, water, and coffee.

8. **Mineral Mix** (magnesium, manganese, phosphorus, selenium, zinc, copper, cobalt, chromium, trace minerals, gold, and fluoride).
You may use only distilled water for washing, drinking, and showering. You may eat only cooked rice, vegetables, fruits, meats, eggs, milk, coffee, and tea. No root vegetables.

9. **Heavy metals** (mercury, lead, cadmium, aluminum, arsenic, copper, gold, silver, and vanadium).
You may use only distilled water for drinking, washing and showering. You may eat only cooked rice, vegetables, fruits, meats, eggs, milk, coffee, and tea.

10. **Salt Mix** (sodium and sodium chloride, water filter water softener salts, and chemicals).
You may use distilled water for drinking and washing, cooked rice, fresh vegetables and fruits (except celery, carrots, beets, artichokes, romaine lettuce, and watermelon) meats, chicken, and sugars.

11. **Corn Mix** (blue corn, yellow corn, cornstarch, cornsilk, corn syrup).
You may eat only steamed vegetables, steamed rice, broccoli, baked chicken, and meats. You may drinkk water, tea and/or coffee without cream or sugar.

12. **Grain Mix** (wheat, gluten, corn, oats, millet, barley, and rice).
You may eat vegetables, fruits, meats, milk, and drink water. Avoid all products with gluten.

11. **Artificial Sweeteners** (Sweet and Low, Equal, saccharine, Twin, and aspartame).
You may eat: anything without artificial sweeteners. Use freshly prepared items only.

12. **Yeast Mix** (brewer's yeast, and bakers yeast).
You may eat vegetables, meat, chicken, and fish. No fruits, no sugar products. Drink distilled water.

13. **Alcohol** (candy, ice cream, liquid medication in alcohol, and alcohol).
You may eat vegetables, meats, fish eggs, and chicken.

14. **Stomach acid** (Hydrochloric acid).
You may eat raw and steamed vegetables, cooked dried beans, eggs, oils, clarified butter, and milk.

15. **Base** (digestive juice from the intestinal tract contains various digestive enzymes: amylase, protease, lipase, maltase, peptidase, bromelain, cellulase, sucrase, papain, lactase, gluco-amylase, and alpha galactosidase).
You may eat: sugars, starches, breads, and meats.

Animal Fats (butter, lard, chicken fat, beef fat, lamb fat, and fiish oil).
You may use anything other than the above including vegetable oils.

Vegetable Fats (corn oil, canola oil, peanut oil, linseed oil, sunflower oil, palm oil, flax seed oil, and coconut oil).
You may use steamed vegetables, steamed rice rice, meats, eggs, chicken, butter, and animal fats.

Vitamin F
You may eat anything that does not contain vegetable oils, wheat germs oils, linseed oil, sunflower oil, soybean oil, safflower oil, peanuts and peanut oil.

Whiten All
You may eat cooked vegetables, pasta, rice, meats, chicken, and eggs.

Food additives (sulfates, nitrates, BHT).
You cannot eat hotdogs or any pre-packaged food. Eat anything made at home from scratch.

Food colors (different food colors in many sources like: ice cream, candy, cookie, gums, drinks, spices, other foods, and/or lipsticks, etc.).
You may eat foods that are freshly prepared. Avoid carrots, natural spices, beets, berries, frozen green leafy vegetables like spinach.

Turkey
You may eat any food that does not contain B1, B3, B6, tryptophane, and neurotransmitters (dopamine, epinephrine, nor-epinephrine, serotonin, acetyl-choline).

Neurotransmitters (dopamine, epinephrine, nor-epinephrine, serotonin, acetyl-choline).
You may eat anything other than milk products, and turkey.

Dried bean Mix (vegetable proteins, soybean, and lecithin).
You may eat rice, pasta, vegetables, meats, eggs, and anything other than beans and bean products.

Amino Acids-1 (essential amino acids: lysine, methionine, leucine, threonine, valine, thryptophane, isoleucine, and phenylalanine).
You may eat cooked white rice, lettuce, and boiled chicken.

Amino Acids 2 (non essential amino acids: alanine, arginine, aspartic acid, carnitine citrulline, cysteine, glutamic acid, glycine, histidine, ornithine, proline, serine, taurine, and tyrosine).
You may eat cooked white rice, boiled beef (corned beef), and iceberg lettuce.

Coffee Mix (coffee, chocolate, caffeine, tannic acid, cocoa, cocoa butter, and carob.
You may eat anything that has no coffee, caffeine, chocolate and/or carob.

Hormones (estrogen, progesterone, testosterone).
You may eat vegetables, fruits, grains, chicken, and fish.

MSG (monosodium glutamate).
You may eat freshly prepared vegetables, fruits, meat, and grains without MSG.

Refined starches (corn starch, potato starch, and modified starch).
You may eat whole grains, vegetables, meats, chicken, and fish.

School work materials (crayons, coloring paper and books, inks, pencils, crayons, glue, play dough, other arts, and craft materials).
Avoid using them or contacting them. Wear a pair of gloves if you have to go near them.

Immunizations and vaccinations either you received or your parent received before you were born (DPT, POLIO, MMR, small pox, chicken pox, influenza, or hepatitis).
Nothing to avoid except infected persons or recently innoculated persons if there are any near you.

Any **drugs given in infancy**, during childhood or taken by the mother during pregnancy (antibiotics, sedatives, laxatives, or recreational drugs).
Avoid the drug.

Fabrics (daily and sleep attire; towels, bed linens, blankets, formaldehyde).
Treat each kind of fabric seperately and avoid the particular cloth or kind of cloth for 25 hours.

Chemicals (chlorine, swimming pool water, detergents, fabric softeners, soaps, cleaning products, shampoos, lipsticks, and cosmetics you or other family members use).

Avoid the above items.

Plastics (toys, play or work materials, utensils, toiletries, computer key boards, and/or phone).

Avoid contact with products made from plastics. Wear a pair of cotton gloves.

Collect different food groups from every meal and treat for the mixture of breakfast, lunch and dinner. Collect this combined food sample at least four times a month and treat using NAET.

The items listed below are treated as needed and on a priority based protocol, which your NAET practitioner will explain to you.

Water (drinking water, tap water, filtered water, city water, lake water, rain water, ocean water, and river water).

People can react to any water. Treat them as needed and avoid the item treated.

Perfume (room deodorizers, soaps, flowers, perfumes, or after-shave, etc.).

Avoid perfume and any fragrance from flowers or products containing perfume.

Baking powder/ Baking soda (in baked goods, toothpaste, and/ or detergents).

You may eat or use anything that does not contain baking powder or baking soda including fresh fruits, vegetables, fats, meat, and chicken.

Other Hormones (histamine, endorphin, enkaphalin, and acetaldehyde).

Avoid touching your own body.

Nut Mix 1 (peanuts, black walnuts, or English walnuts).

You may eat any foods that do not contain the nuts listed above including their oils and butter.

Nut Mix 2: (cashew, almonds, pecan, Brazil nut, hazelnut, macadamia nut, and sunflower seeds).
You may eat any foods that do not contain the nuts listed above including their oils and butters.

Spice Mix 1: (ginger, cardamonnn, cinnamon cloves, nutmeg, garlic, cumin, fennel, coriander, turmeric, saffron, and mint).
You may use all foods and products without these items.

Spice Mix 2 (peppers, red pepper, black pepper, green pepper, jalapeno, banana peppers, anise seed, basil, bay leaf, caraway seed, chervil, cream of tartar, dill, fenugreek, horseradish, mace, MSG, mustard, onion, oregano, paprika, poppy seed, parsley, rosemary, sage, sumac, and vinegar).
You may eat or use all foods and food products without the above listed spices.

Fish Mix (Cod, halibut, salmon, shark, and tuna).
You may eat any food that does not contain the fish or fish oils listed above.

Shellfish Mix (Shrimp, lobster, abalone, cray, crab, and clams).
You may eat any food that does not contain fish products.

Whey
You may eat rice, vegetables, fruits, chicken, egg, turkey, beef, pork, beans, and lamb.

Yogurt
You may eat rice, vegetables, fruits, poultry, and meat.

Gelatin

You may use anything that does not contain gelatin.

Gum Mix (Acacia, Karaya gum, Xanthiane gum, black gum, sweet gum, and chewing gum).
You may eat rice, pasta, vegeatables, fruits without skins, meats, eggs, and chicken, drink juice and water.

Paper Products (newspaper, newspaper ink, reading books, coloring books, books with colored illustrations)
Avoid the above items.

Fluoride You may use or eat: fruits, poultry, meat, potato, cauliflower, white rice, and yellow vegeatables.You may use distilled water, drink fresh fruit juices.

Vitamin E
You may eat fresh fish, carrots, potato, poultry, and meat.

Vitamin D
You may eat fruits, vegeatbles, poultry, and meats.

VitaminK
You may eat fish, rice, potato, poultry, and meat.

Night shade vegetables (bell pepper, onion, eggplant, potato, tomato (fruits, sauces, and drinks).
Avoid eating these vegetables.

Pesticides (malathion, termite control items, or regular pesticides).
Avoid meats, grasses, ant sprays, and pesticides.

Insect bites in infancy or childhood (bee stings, spider bites, or cockroach, etc.).
Treat for the individual insect and avoid it while treating.

Latex products (shoe, sole of the shoe, elastic, rubber bands, and/or rubber bathtub toys).
Avoid latex products.

Radiation (computer, television, microwave, X-ray, and the sun).
Avoid radiation of any kind.

Inhalants
Avoid pollens, weeds, grasses, flowers, wood mix, room air, outside air, smog, and polluted air from nearby factories.

Tissues and secretions (DNA, RNA, thyroid hormone, pituitary hormone, pineal gland, hypothalamus, or brain tissue, liver, blood, and saliva).

Treat these items individually if needed. Avoid touching your own body. Wear a pair of gloves for 25 hours.

Allergies to people, animals and pets (mother, father, care takers, cats, and dogs).
Avoid the ones you were treated for 25 hours.

Emotional allergies (fear, fright, frustration, anger, low self-esteem, and/or rejection, etc.).
Nothing to avoid for emotional treatment.

After clearing the allergy to nutrients, appropriate supplementation with vitamins, minerals, and enzymes etc., is necessary to make up the deficiency and promote healing. Please read the guidebook for information on how to take supplent correctly.

Your NAET doctor will also do a few energy boosting techniques with vitamin B complex, calcium, vitamin F, neurotransmitters, sugar, trace minerals, and magnesium.

THE NEUROTOXINS

There are many substances that can irritate brain function, especially when taken on a daily basis. Most people are unaware of the symptoms these substances can cause in the body.

Artificial Sweeteners
There are many kinds of artificial sweeteners available today, which are refined and can effect and irritate the brain.

Caffeine, Coffee, Chocolate
A caffeine- like substance is secreted by certain parts of the brain, which is very essential for its normal function. If the child is allergic to any of these, it can irritate the brain.

Night-shade Vegetables
Tomato, potato, eggplant, bell pepper and onion make up the nightshade vegetable group. Most people are missing the enzyme in their bodies that help digest the special chemical contained in these vegetables. After treatment and clearance, the body will begin to make the special enzyme to digest these vegetables.

Alcohol
Whether or not you drink alcohol, your body needs it. Alcohol is made from refined starches and other form of sugars. Many people are allergic to sugar and thus alcohol.

Refined Starches
Refined starches are used as a thickening agent in sauces and drinks. Many people are allergic to starches. Refined starches should be avoided.

NAET STUDY ON ADD/ADHD PATIENTS

A statistical study done on 138 people, (18 females-13.1%; 120 males-86.9%) between the ages of 4-46, having 13-55 NAET treatments over a five-year-period showed:

94.2% were absolutely free of drugs. (130 people are not taking any medication. They are absolutely free of symptoms).

4.3% reported to be about 70 % better overall with their symptoms. These six people suffer from other mental disorders and have to take a low dose of medication.

1.5% reported 30-50 % improvement overall.

These two people are still taking Ritalin or similar drugs, unable to get off medication due to other mental disorders, but reported an overall feeling of well being. They were allergic to drugs initially, causing violent behavior. After the treatments for drugs, they were able to take drugs to reduce or control other symptoms.

Books to read on NAET
by Devi S. Nambudripad, D.C. L.Ac., R.N., O.M.D., Ph.D.

Say Good-bye To Illness
Living Pain Free with Acupressure
The NAET Guide Book
Say Good-bye to ADD and ADHD

CHAPTER ELEVEN

NAET - ADHD
CASE
STUDIES

11

NAET - ADHD CASE STUDIES

I have treated many cases in each category from the list given above. Most people think ADHD applies only to children, but that is not true. ADHD probably begins in childhood. When these children grow up without removing their childhood problems, they become ADHD adults. It can begin at any age, as you will see in some case studies on the following pages. From the hundreds of cases I have treated with NAET, I believe the major cause of ADHD in children and adults is some type of allergy. Find the allergen for the particular individual using MRT (Chapter 6) and before you know it, you can say "Good-Bye to ADHD." I hope the following unique case studies will help you to become a better detective in locating your own problems.

1. **EGG MIX** (egg white, egg yolk, chicken, and tetracycline). You may need to test them individually for allergies after completing the group treatment for egg mix. If they need to be treated individually, treat them individually before beginning the second treatment (calcium mix).

27-year-old Simon came in with a unique complaint. He worked as salesman at an auto dealership. He reported to work every day by 8am. As soon as he began his work, he felt highly

irritable and would have a queasy feeling in his stomach. Sometimes he also felt nervous and panicky for no particular reason. He
was very tired and suffered from dull body ache and joint pains
throughout the day, mainly in the morning. He didn't like morn-
ings any more. All of these symptoms and discomfort lasted until
10:30 A.M. Then he usually was fine for the rest of the day.
Occasionally, his symptoms returned at night for a few hours. Whenever he felt nervous he also needed to keep moving his legs to
make him feel slightly better (restless legs). If he was sitting, he
needed to rock his body and legs back and forth, otherwise he felt
as if his circulation was going to stop. People around him became
irritated, but he did not know how to control his restlessness. He
was given certain drugs to calm his nerves but they didn't seem to
work on him. He continued having the same problem practically
every day. Names of drugs will not be mentioned here, because it
is not the drug that is at fault, an allergy to the drug is usually the
reason it doesn't work. It is not necessary to develop a fear to any
particular drug.

He was brought up on a farm and suffered from eczema,
asthma, lack of energy, attention deficit disorders and was dys-
lexic in his childhood. But he outgrew the dyslexia and asthma.
When he became a teenager, his eczema got better; however, he
began having a nervous stomach and bowels, restless body and
legs, and anxiety attacks. It was hard for him to go through the
school. He couldn't concentrate or pay attention to the teacher. He
always experienced a butterfly sensation in his stomach. He felt as
if the world was going to come to an end in few hours. He was
admitted to the hospital for panic attacks when he was 14 years
old. His dream was to become a college professor one day, but he
couldn't do well in school. Somehow he managed to graduate from
high school.

His family history showed that his father, a farmer, suffered
from arthritis and eczema all his life. His mother had anxiety disorders and an uncle suffered from asthma.

He ate one boiled egg every day for breakfast with a slice of dry wheat toast and a glass of skim milk. He took a multiple vitamin with a glass of water. He ate a salad for lunch without dressing. He ate boiled rice, steamed vegetables, Jell-O pudding or egg custard for dinner. He drank 6 glasses of purified water every day. He was trying to eat a healthy diet. He was a vegetarian except for the one egg that he ate for protein every day.

In our office, he was tested through NTT and found to be highly allergic to eggs and chicken. He was slightly allergic to vegetables but not allergic to boiled rice. NTT confirmed that egg caused a severe energy blockage in his lungs (asthma), stomach (nervous stomach, anxiety disorders, etc.), spleen (general body ache, fatigue, etc.), liver (irritability, restlessness, etc.), and colon meridians (restless leg syndrome, eczema, nervous bowels, etc.). He was surprised at this discovery. He reminded us that he was brought up in a farm, where they grew chickens. He was fed on eggs and chicken practically every day ever since he was an infant.

He was advised to stay away from egg and egg products for a week. We asked him to write down the changes he noticed every day and return in a week. He noticed the difference within two days. He stopped having a nervous stomach, restless legs, and irritability. He was not fatigued and his body and joints ached less. I asked him if he could eat an egg that day and return on the following day. He did and said that his symptoms all returned an hour after eating the egg. He ate his favorite egg custard that night and his symptoms were reproduced. This answered his question about occasional night time restlessness. But this time he noticed his symptoms were stronger than before.

When you abstain from an allergen, your symptoms should disappear in a specific amount of time. After few days of avoidance, when you reintroduce the allergen, especially a severe one, your symptoms could be worse. When he returned on the following day, he was treated with NAET for eggs and chicken. Now he can eat eggs three times a day and egg custard every night without causing any unpleasant symptoms. Ever since that first NAET treatment he said, he experienced a general feeling of well being. He does not have nervous stomach, nervous legs, body and joint pains, general fatigue, and anxiety attacks any more.

Simon was lucky, with just one NAET treatment, he felt as if he got back control of his life. It doesn't usually happen this way to every one. Most people are allergic to many things around them. They need to get treated for at least 10-20 basic groups before they notice differences in their health, because we use about 10-20 food groups in our daily diet. Simon was allergic mainly to eggs and his allergy to vegetable wasn't a big one. He was not allergic to boiled rice. He ate a minimum number of food groups every day. He was not allergic to many chemicals. He was not allergic to the environment. Actually he was not allergic to many other things in his living or work environment. He was also wise to maintain a fairly clean diet, and drank an adequate amount of water, and exercised regularly. This gave him a better immune system. Even with all that good living, his body could not handle the allergic effect of the one egg he ate daily. The egg in his daily diet could have contributed to his childhood suffering. If his parents only knew how to test for allergy to eggs by NTT, he might have had a different life.

2. MILK AND CALCIUM (breast milk, cow's milk, goat's milk, and calcium). You may need to test them individually for allergies after completing the group treatment for calcium mix. If they need to be treated individually, treat them individually before you begin the group number three (vitamin C).

Michael, six- years-old, was suffering from ADD. He could not sit in the class quietly even for a few minutes. He constantly moved around jumping, climbing on the bench, running around the room and tearing coloring books, etc. His school refused to keep him in the class if he was not placed on calming drugs. His parents were desperate. He was finally put on drugs. But instead of calming down, his condition got worse. He began acting violent and impossible. His parents were advised to enroll him in a special school for such children. That's when his mother heard about NAET from another parent. He was brought to our office immediately and began NAET treatments. He was highly allergic to milk and milk products. In less than 6 treatments, Michael calmed down naturally. After 14 treatments, Michael was tested again and was better than ever before. He was admitted once again to his regular school.

3. VITAMIN C (vitamin C, ascorbic acid, oxalic acid, rutin, hespiridin, bioflavonoids). You may need to test them individually for allergies after completing the group treatment for vitamin C mix. If they need to be treated individually, treat them individually before the next group of treatment (B complex group).

A 32-year-old registered nurse, an ex-patient, came to our office with complaints of depression that had originally started one week earlier. She began crying desperately. She said she didn't see any need to live any longer. She felt worthless and unloved. Kinesiological testing revealed that the home-canned apples she had been eating for the past week caused her depression. The canned apples came from her mother's house in northern California. Her mother had canned them for her. In this case, she was allergic to the apples, which in turn affected her liver, and caused a blockage in the liver meridian. When she was treated for the apples, the depression was gone.

4. B COMPLEX VITAMINS (15 B-vitamins - B1, B2, B3, B4, B5, B6, (folic acid), B12, B13, B15, B17, Biotin, Paba, choline, inositol). You may need to test them individually for allergies after completing the group treatment for mineral mix. If they need to be treated individually, treat them individually before the fifth group of treatment (sugar mix).

Randy, 33-year-old male, presented us with a long list of problems on his first day in our office. He had suffered from these problems for six years. Before that he did not have any health problems. He grew up and lived in a rural area until six years ago. Then he moved to the big city for his employment. He was single and lived alone.

His major complaints were anger, irritability, restlessness, insecurity, mood swings, insomnia, joint pains, depression, paranoia, and low self-esteem. He worked in a computer software company where he had hundreds of people working with him. He always felt others were judging him and talking about him every time they looked at him. This made him very uneasy all the time. He felt that he was not good enough for anything and was startled easily by any tiny sound or movement.

He recognized his weakness and reached for help. He was given special medication to calm him down and relax. He felt sleepy with the drugs and he could not work efficiently. One of his friends suggested some natural cures for his problems. He began reading about natural resources to conquer his problem. From reading books he associated his symptoms with a calcium deficiency in his diet. He began drinking a couple of glasses of milk a day. Instead of getting better, his symptoms got worse. His joints hurt more severely. Then one day he read about NAET on the web site. He was intrigued by the information and immediately made an appointment. He was highly allergic to all the basic food groups, which caused energy blockages in all 12 meridians. We immediately began NAET, and as soon as he completed the calcium treatment, his joint pains eased. B complex, sugar, salt and mineral treatments helped him with depression, paranoia, restlessness, mood swings, and anger. Iron helped him with his long-term insomnia.

He was alo allergic to various chemicals, computer keyboards, computer monitors, carpets, and formaldehyde. After completing 50-60 treatments, he was a new man. He enjoyed being in the world once again, doing his work and working with others without having any feelings of paranoia. Most likely, the scientific discoveries and the chemical pollution of the city life caused blockages in his energy meridians leaving him dysfunctional in the city.

A 49-year-old schoolteacher suffered from severe clinical depression for a couple of years. She was seeing a psychologist regularly and taking antidepressants. Nothing seemed to help her. She was referred to our office and found to be allergic to grains, sugars, B vitamins, pesticides, make-up materials, detergents and soaps, which caused blockages in the stomach and liver meridians. After she was treated for the above items, she was asked to take large amounts (15 times the daily dosage) of B complex vitamins. In a few days, her depression was reduced immensely. She continued to take B vitamins for a few months. When her B complex requirement was met, she became normal again.

5. SUGAR MIX (cane sugar, corn sugar, maple sugar, grape sugar, rice sugar, beet sugar, brown sugar, molasses, honey, dextrose, glucose, maltose). You may need to test them individually for allergies after completing the group treatment for mineral mix. If they need to be treated individually, treat them individually before the next treatments.

Sugar is indeed a magic nutrient. But it is a mistaken and misunderstood nutrient in today's world. Sugar is essential in the body for various enzymatic functions and to help B-vitamins accomplish their functions in the body. If we are not allergic to sugar, we do not have to eat sugar as white sugar, brown sugar, honey, molasses, fructose, dextrose, glucose, grape sugar, rice sugar, beet sugar, malt sugar, etc. We can eat any type of food and the body will convert the raw materials into sugar for its use. If we eat sugar as in above sugar form, the body will use what it needs and will throw the rest out. Some patients crave sugar before the NAET treatment; a few days after the treatment, they don't even miss it. Before the treatment, the body was not able to assimilate sugar even when the person ate a lot of sugar; the cells were not getting sugar. The body was demanding sugar but it didn't have any left in storage for everyday use.

When the person craves sugar, he/she is going to eat it and the body will assimilate a tiny portion of consumed sugar by osmosis for its use. But after the treatment, when the body assimilates sugar through proper channels, the body doesn't demand sugar anymore so the patient doesn't crave sugar any more. That is how the allergy works. If we have an allergy towards an essential nutrient like sugar, we crave that substance. When we have no allergy, our bodies are happy and craving subsides. So when someone says sugar is bad for you, it doesn't mean anything to us. If you are allergic to it then it is bad, otherwise it is good.

6. **IRON MIX** (animal and vegetable sources, beef, pork, lamb, raisin, dates, and broccoli).

Mike, nine-years-old, was brought to the office for hyperactive behavior, unreasonable anger, agitation, poor attention span, and behavioral problems. According to the mother, Mike was a good boy and behaved normally on some days, but on certain days he was very wild. He was tested through NTT and found to be allergic to almost all the common foods. We began treatments. He did great with the treatments and he behaved almost normally through the treatment for the sugar group. When he was treated for the iron group, he became very violent and lost his temper at another younger child-patient in the office. His unusual behavior gave us the clue that he did not receive the treatment correctly. His face looked stiff, his eyes looked angry. He failed to calm down. We tested him through a surrogate again and found that he still had blockages in his heart, liver and stomach meridians. He refused to cooperate to receive NAET. Finally he had to be treated through a surrogate (his mother). He was treated with NAET again for three more times every ten minutes. At the end of the third treatment, his face relaxed and he appeared calm. He apologized at his mother's request to the other child-patient with whom he misbehaved earlier. He was a changed boy from the next visit on. He ate hamburger three times a week and his mother thought the reason for his misbehavior was the allergy to the hamburger.

7. VITAMIN A MIX (animal and vegetable source, beta carotene, fish, and shellfish).

Gary, twelve-years-old, came to our office with complaints of repeated migraine headaches for three years. His mother was a firm believer in healthy eating and sent carrot sticks to school with him for his snack every day. He would eat the carrot sticks about ten o'clock and drink purified water. Ten minutes after his morning snack, his headache would begin and peak in less than a half an hour. Whenever he had the headache, he would become agitated and angry with the other children. His behavior became intolerable. The teacher would call his mother for a conference and he would be sent home. This happened continually. His mother took him to the doctor. He was diagnosed as having migraines and was sent home with medication.

When Gary came to our office, he was still on regular medication for migraine headaches. He continued to have migraines even though he was taking the medication daily. He would wake up with a mild headache and continued to have dull headaches throughout the day. Some days he would get excruciating headaches at school. He was treated for the basics, which included vitamin A mix. The day after the treatment for vitamin A mix, Gary came to the office with a big smile. He told us that he didn't have a trace of a headache the whole day after the treatment. That was his turning point. In this case the beta-carotene and vitamin A in the carrots he was eating every day induced his migraine headaches and aggressive behavior!

Margaret was 39 when she discovered NAET through a friend. She came in complaining of severe stomach cramps every night for the past 5 years, whether she ate any food or not. She also suffered from severe insomnia, anger and irritability. She saw a gastro-enterologist, (diseases of the digestive tract), and took variety of lab tests, and X-rays. The doctor could not find any abnormalities. She tried different practitioners of healing arts to get some relief from her annoying symptom. She took drugs, herbs and homeopathic remedies, but nothing gave her any satisfactory result.

In our office, we found out through NTT that she was very allergic to vitamin A mix and fish group, which caused a severe energy blockage in the stomach meridian (stomachache) and liver meridian (anger, irritability, and insomnia). But she claimed that she was a strict vegetarian. She never even touched fish or anything made with fish in her lifetime. She never liked carrots or spinach and had never eaten them for years. I could see on her face that she wasn't convinced with my finding. Checking her food and supplement list, we discovered that five years ago she began taking oyster shell calcium which was prescribed by her doctor for her calcium deficiency and to prevent osteoporosis. She took it every night. When she thought about it, she remembered experiencing stomach discomfort the very first night she took the pill. She was advised to stay away from the pill for a week and then return for re-evaluation. She returned after a week still having stomach discomfort, but it was less in-

Say Good-bye to ADD and ADHD

Dear Doctor Devi,

I am writing to let you know that how pleased I am at the results of your examination and NAET treatment on my son, Nick, on August 10 through 14, 1998. My son had been diagnosed with attention-deficit hyperactive disorder, and was taking Ritalin by prescription from his pediatrician. The Ritalin was not producing the results that I desired, so, in a desperate attempt to help him, I sought out and turned to a natural method. I had also observed that he did not react well to processed sugar. Specifically, I observed that within 20-30 minutes of drinking soda or eating candy, he became excessively energetic and was unable to focus on anything for more than a few minutes. As you recall, I brought him to you for examination and testing with regards to these problems.

On August 12th, you tested him for allergies and discovered a strong allergy to sugar ... up to a distance of approximately five feet! I was present during the testing and personally witnessed the results. If I understood you correctly, your test also indicated that his brain was producing too much energy. You performed the NAET procedure which, I'm told, is designed to clear allergies from the body. I was present before and after the procedure. I was not allowed to stand in the same room while he was being treated to avoid the interference with his magnetic field. After his treatment we waited in your office for the next 20 minutes, then my son was asked to

192

wash his hands with plain water to remove the energy of the sugar from his hands. My son had to abstain from sugar in any form for 25 hours after the procedure was finished in order for it to work. All foods containing sugar, including packaged food, fruit, etc., were put away in closed cabinets, and I followed a list of permitted foods for his diet for the next 25 hours. He was allowed to eat white rice, vegetables, chicken, eggs, vegetable oil, salt, and water to drink. Honestly Doctor, it wasn't easy, but we survived the 25 hours. And now, without any hesitation, I am ecstatic with the results! The day after the procedure was finished for the sugar, my son ate three sweet rolls at church- the kind with the white sugary icing on top. I was completely amazed: he remained completely calm. If this had been two weeks earlier that much sugar would have left him bouncing like a rubber ball! One of our church members even commented on how "subdued" he had been during service, and asked if he was tired. I explained to her what we had done at your office. She was a bit surprised, after all, this is the first time she had heard about the NAET procedure. Nevertheless, she said, "Well, it works! So who am I to doubt it? Doctor, I can't thank you enough. Since that day in Church, I have seen many more instances to corroborate the results of the NAET. The bottom line: Nick is no longer allergic to sugar! Thank you for the tiny miracle that has made a huge impact on one boy's life.

Thankfully yours,
Happy Mom.

tense. She did not take the pills, but left the pill bottle (glass) sitting at the side table near her bed. She was willing to research this further agreed not to use the pill for another week. She went home and put away the pills in a closed wooden cabinet. She slept better that night without any discomfort. She waited for three more nights and she still did not have any discomfort whatsoever.

She was convinced this time. She returned and went through the complete NAET program. Vitamin A mix and fish were included in the program. When she finished her treatments, she became healthy again.

8. MINERALS MIX (magnesium, manganese, phosphorus, selenium, zinc, copper, cobalt, chromium, trace minerals, gold, and fluoride). You may need to test them individually for allergies after completing the group treatment for mineral mix. If they need to be treated individually, treat them individually after 20 basic treatments.

Mineral deficiencies, caused both by poor nutritional intake as well as by allergies to these minerals, are a significant contributing factor in ADHD. Statistics show that 100% of these children are deficient in magnesium, 50% are deficient in manganese, and 80% are deficient in zinc. Supplementation is much more effective after clearing the allergies by NAET.

Eleven-year-old Mark had frequent nightmares, wet the bed, sucked his thumb, and constantly moved around. He was allergic to many food products and chemicals. But when we treated him for the trace minerals, suddenly his condition changed. The day after he was treated for minerals, he was dry when he woke up. Through the day, his mother noticed changes in him. After 25 hours of the treatment, he appeared very calm and settled. He continued to get more NAET treatments: food colors, food additives, pesticides, formaldehyde, fabrics, fabric softeners, and plastics. He now is a sensible productive teen-ager.

9. SALT AND CHLORIDE (sodium and sodium chloride, water filter/ water softener salts, and chemicals). In some patients, you may need to treat them individually. Individual treatments should be done after 20 basic treatments.

Twenty-one-year-old, Suzy had been a good student throughout high school and college. She was preparing to be a lawyer. Suddenly something happened to her mentally and she lost interest and motivation in her studies. She felt depressed and sad for no particular reason. She fought with her boy friend and they separated. She felt tingly all over the body. Her mind wandered, she had trouble concentrating; she had trouble sleeping. She was found to be allergic to iodized salt. Today, after being treated for all the basics and iodized salt, she is a practicing attorney and is symptom-free.

10. GRAIN MIX (wheat, gluten, corn, oats, millet, barley, rice).You may need to test and treat them individually. If needed treat them before the next item.

A 59-year-old man had frequent headaches for the past few years. His headaches were severe after the consumption of any grain. It was discovered through kinesiological testing that he had a financial loss when he was 41. He lost his restaurant business and was very sad about it. He may have been eating breads and grain products while he was grieving for the financial loss, and his confused brain assumed that eating the grain and grain products made him sad. Thus with any future contact with grains, his brain began giving warning signals such as migraine headaches. After the treatment for the incident, he no longer had the usual headaches.

11. **YEAST MIX** (brewer's yeast, bakers yeast).

41-year-old Marcia had a strange problem. Whenever she had anything with yeast (bread) or a sip of alcohol her feet swelled up blistered and itched all over. She couldn't sleep and became very hyper and moody. She also had shooting pains inside her head for a couple of days. By the second day, her feet began to ooze serum from the blisters. She had to take off from work and stay home for the next few days whenever she had anything with yeast or alcohol. After the basics, she was treated with NAET for yeast mix, followed by alcohol mix. Her health improved after the alcohol treatment.

12. **STOMACH ACID** (Hydrochloric acid).

Sonia, 24-year-old, suffered from bulimia for four years. She tried different treatments. Then she was sent to our office. During NTT evaluation, she told me that ten minutes after eating anything, she felt highly acidic and she had to thow up to feel relieved. She was allergic to her stomach acid. She was treated for stomach acid immediately and was sent home. The next week when she returned to our office, she looked very happy. According to her, her acid reflux and bulimia stopped the next day after the treatment for stomach acid. Treatment for bulimia was that easy for Sonia, but this is one case in a million. People with bulimia shouldn't get overexcited reading Sonia's story. Because each patient's individual case is different.

13. **BASE** (digestive juice from the intestinal tract contains various digestive enzymes: amylase, protease, lipase, maltase, peptidase, bromelain, cellulase, sucrase, papain, lactase, gluco-amylase, and alpha galactosidase).

Tom, fifteen-years-old, complained of severe abdominal bloating for two-three hours after he ate a normal meal. It was very uncomfortable. He became very irritable and angry towards everyone. He suffered from insomnia and couldn't fall asleep until three o'clock in the morning. He had to wake up by six o'clock to get to school on time. He began dreading to eat food. He was allergic to alkalinity of his intestinal juices; not being able to produce enough digestive juices to help digest the food he was eating. When he was successfully treated for Base (intestinal digestive juices), his abdominal bloating stopped.

14. DRINKING WATER / TAP WATER

Melissa, who was seven-years-old, had developed hyperactivity and restlessness along with eczema nine months before her mother brought her to us for evaluation and treatment. Testing by NTT revealed that she was suffering from an allergy to water. Her mother had installed a new water filtration system nine months ago. The water softener was the culprit causing her irritability and eczema. When she was successfully treated for the water, she was no longer hyperactive and her skin became normal.

15. FATS (animal fat, vegetable fat, butter, oils, and fatty acids)

People with irritable nervous system (ADHD and children with other brain disorders) use up essential fatty acid rapidly. So this deficiency is quite common in ADHD patients and often requires supplementation with good fatty acid after clearing the allergy.

Moran, fourteen-years-old, suffered from attention deficit disorders since childhood. He also suffered from severe painful acne and dry skin. He was taking medication to reduce his ADHD since the age of four. He was found to be allergic to all the basic 18 groups of foods. When he completed the treatment for vitamin A, his hyperactivity reduced slightly. But he continued to have acne and boils on his face. When he was treated for fats, his acne and dry skin improved. After clearing for the basic groups, he was no longer hyperactive and functioned normally in school and home.

15. **DRIED BEANS** (vegetable proteins, soybean, lecithin).

Dried beans are also considered harmless, natural proteins. But if you are allergic to them, they can cause severe reactions. Ron, 16-years-old, came to us with severe low backache. Testing with NTT revealed that lentil soup he had eaten the day before caused his backache. He was successfully treated for dried beans and within half an hour he was free of his backache.

16. **Caffeine mix** (chocolate, coffee smell and taste, caffeine, soft drinks).

Michael, a 37-year old school teacher liked coffee. He drank 6-8 cups daily. Whenever he felt tired, he would make a pot of coffee and drink a couple of cups. His energy would return and he would be able to finish his work for the day. But lately, he felt tired more often, needing to increase his coffee intake even more, to 12-14 cups daily. He also developed a few dermatological problems. He started itching all over his body: on his face, the sides of his cheeks, in front of his ears and his skin began to peel off. Then he went to see a dermatologist. All the medicines and topical creams he received helped him temporarily. He had to take medication to get to sleep. He started to put on weight in spite of all the tennis he played. He began worrying about his health. He still kept drinking coffee. One day while he was browsing through the Internet for a solution for his itching, he read about NAET and allergies. NAET mentioned about addiction to coffee and immediately he saw the link between his health problems and the enormous amount of coffee he was drinking. He tried to stop drinking coffee for a day. His body trembled and his limbs turned cold and clammy. He felt extremely tired, became depressed, lost all motivation, and started getting body aches and joint pains. Finally, in the evening he drank a couple of cups of coffee and felt better. By then he realized that he had become addicted to coffee.

When he came to see me he was quite desperate. He felt embarrassed for becoming a coffee addict. He began NAET treatment right away. In five treatments (egg mix, calcium mix, vitamin C mix, B complex mix and sugar mix), his coffee cravings stopped, but he continued to have other symptoms. With every treatment his condition improved. When he finished all the basic NAET treatments including coffee, he became normal again. Now he is satisfied with one cup of coffee per day.

17. Artificial Sweeteners (Sweet and Low, Equal, saccharine, Twin, and aspartame).

Jay was six when he was seen in our office for severe frequent headaches, aggressive behaviors, anger and sibling rivalry. He had one older brother who was ten and a younger sister who was four. He did not like either one. He often bit his brother and beat up his little sister. One night, his brother had to be rushed to the hospital because Jay bit a piece out of his thigh and it began bleeding. If he did not get what he wanted immediately, he began biting people. His friends kept away from him. His brother refused to play with him and his sister was afraid of him. The school refused to admit him. His father and mother felt embarrassed and worried about him. He was placed on Ritalin. He began to have a fever and he broke out in huge hives. His parents took him to a child psychologist who treated him for a few months. But nothing seemed to help with his behavior problems. Jay was singled out, and the other two children joined together and fought with him all the time. His mother was tired of solving the arguments and fights between the siblings, giving them punishments and times-out; but, his father did not want to interfere. Finally they thought they had had enough, he was too disruptive to have him in their home anymore. They were ready to give him up for adoption. Her husband decided that they would have to be satisfied with two healthy children; the third one would have to find another home, without any other children to make him unhappy. He told her this was the best for Jay and the family.

Jay's mother was not very healthy either. She suffered from severe migraines for four years. She took many prescription pills and herbs daily. But she continued to get the migraines at least once a day. One of her friends suggested NAET to her to control her migraines and she came in and began NAET treatments immediately.

She continued to have migraines through B complex mix. But during her sugar treatment (the fifth one), she had a crying spell due to an emotional blockage. Through NTT, I traced her emotional blockage to her children. In the midst of tears and sobbing, she described the troubled situation in her family. I suggested to her that she should bring Jay in for a few NAET treatments. After her sugar treatment, she said good-bye to her migraines.

We began NAET on Jay. He responded well to the treatments. With each treatment, he began showing signs of improvement. Each one of the treatments was difficult for him because he needed to avoid the allergen being treated for a good thirty hours (his allergy was so severe). His headaches were better after seven treatments.

Then one day he came to the office accompanied by his mother complaining of a severe headache. His headache started after he ate a home-made cookie. One of the ingredients was a natural sweetener. Jay was highly allergic to this particular product. His mother said that she used this product in her cooking a lot since it had no calories. She fed her children and her husband this natural sweetener ever since she discovered it four years ago. Jay was treated for this product for five days in a row. His system was saturated with this neurotoxin and it took five consecutive treatments to clear it from his body. During the five days, life in that family was impossible. Trying to take care of this unfriendly, destructive little monster was more than they could bare. Finally, on the sixth day, when Jay woke up his mother knew that he had passed the treatment because Jay was a different child. He had changed into a friendly lovable child.

The allergic sweetener was the cause of four years of misery in the Jackson family. Jay was treated for a few more allergies to his siblings, mother, pets, coloring books, crayons, etc., and his personality turned around. He became the most admirable child in the family. His siblings loved him and friends accepted him. The family did not have to give him up for adoption. Jay is a friendly, happy, bright teenager now. His mother never had another migraine after the sugar treatment that was done eight years ago.

18. FOOD ADDITIVES (sulfates, nitrates, BHT, MSG/ accent, whitenall, gum mix, gelatin). You may need to test them individually for allergies after completing the group treatment for food additives. If they need to be treated individually, treat them individually after 20 basic treatments.

Stan got hyper and suffered from behavioral problems, especially on Monday morning. His parents took him to the beach every Sunday evening and he ate a hotdog from the hotdog stand. He would become very hyper the rest of the evening. He was allergic to the food additives in the hot dog.

19. FOOD COLORS (different food colors in many sources like: ice cream, candy, cookie, gums, drinks, spices, other foods, lipsticks, etc.).

Twelve-year-old Greg, couldn't relax at any time. Even in his sleep, he would restlessly roll back and forth. He had frequent nightmares, wet the bed, and also sucked his thumb. He was allergic to many chemicals, food colors, and additives. His favorite foods were jelly beans, Jello puddings, ice creams, and candies. He craved

He craved these items all the time. He suffered from severe sinusitis Monday through Friday, but felt better Saturday and Sunday. Monday evening his sinuses clogged up again. He fought this problem ever since he started going to school. He was examined by an allergist and received allergy shots for a few years. But his problems persisted. After treatment for food colorings, food additives, ice creams, artificial sweeteners, coloring books, crayons, and MSG, his sinuses cleared up and his behavioral problems and restlessness diminished. He is a responsible, level-headed teenager now.

20. NEUROTRANSMITTERS (amino acids, DNA, RNA, serotonin, GABA, dopamine, epinephrine, nor-epinephrine, histamine, endorphin, enkaphalin, acetyl-choline, and acetaldehyde).

Allergies to neurotransmitters must be identified and treated, including GABA (often associated in hyperactivity), serotonin (distractibility, sleep disturbances and depression), dopamine (poor attention span), epinephrine, norepinephrine (impulsivity).

Heavymetal mix (mercury, lead, cadmium, aluminum, arsenic, copper, gold, silver, zinc, and vanadium). You may need to test them individually for allergies after completing the group treatment for heavymetals. If they need to be treated individually, treat them individually after 20 basic treatments.

These heavy metals are known to be toxic and they affect the brain functions and behavior. When one is allergic to the heavy metals, they tend to accumulate in the unwanted places, esp. in the brain and nervous system causing damages to these areas. ALCAT blood test or hair analysis can detect the presence of these toxins in the blood. NAET to these metals can eliminate the allergy and eventually they will leave the body. A good detox program is advisable after NAET for these metals to achieve faster clearing of the heavy metals from the body.

A simple remedy to detox heavymetals is to drink one ounce of raw potato juice once a day in empty stomach This followed by an ounce of aloevera jell in 30 minutes (no food for half an hour following the drink). 4-6 glasss of water through the day between meals. Do it for a month.

John, 38-year-old, had depression for most of his life. He had tried various treatments, including psychotherapy. He was found to be allergic to cadmium, one of the ingredients seen in coffee. John drank at least ten cups of coffee a day. The stronger the better. He was also allergic to iron. He had wrought-iron ornamental works all over his house. When he was treated for iron, and cadmium his depression cleared

HISTAMINE
Any time there is an allergic reaction in the body, special cells (mast cells) release histamine. One can be allergic to one's own histamine. If one happens to be allergic to histamine, then histamine is produced very frequently in the body. It doesn't stop until the mechanism is turned off or another way to turn off is to take anti-histamine. Vitamin C is natural anti-histamine, that is, if you are not allergic to it. It is very easy to treat with NAET one's own histamine and let the body adjust it to a normal level.

Everyone thinks that turkey is a harmless low cholesterol, lean meat. Turkey is the precursor to serotonin. Many people get very hyper by eating turkey because it has the important neurotransmitter called serotonin. If you are allergic to serotonin, you can suffer from poor concentration and brain irritability. Allergy to serotonin causes depression in sensitive people. This probably explains why there is an increase in suicidal attempts, depression and mental instability around holidays like Thanksgiving, Christmas, and New Year when turkey is usually served.

FABRICS
(daily and sleep attire; towels, bed linens, blankets, and form-aldehyde).

Jane was 32 when she discovered NAET through a friend. She came in complaining of severe stomach cramps every night for the past 2 years, whether she ate any food or not. She also suffered from severe insomnia, anger and irritability. She saw a gastro-enterologist, (diseases of the digestive tract), took barium meal and all other prescribed lab tests and X-rays. The doctor could not find any abnormalities. She tried different practitioners of healing arts to get some relief from her annoying symptom. She took drugs, herbs and homeopathic remedies, but nothing gave her any satisfactory result.

In our office, we found out through NTT that she was very alergic to egg mix, which caused a severe energy blockage in the somach meridian (stomachache) and liver meridian (anger, irritablity, and insomnia). But she claimed that she was a strict vegetarian. She never even touched egg or anything made with egg in her lifetime. I could see on her face that she wasn't convinced with my finding. Checking her household items, we discovered that two years ago she received a feather comforter as a gift from some one very dear to her. She liked the feeling of the feather comforter and used it every day. When she thought about it, she remembered experiencing stomach discomfort the very first night she used the comforter. NAET egg mix sample includes egg white, egg yolk, feather, and tetracycline. She was advised to stay away from the comforter for a week and we asked her to return for re-evaluation. She returned after a week still having stomach discomfort, but it was less intense. She had put the comforter in another room, but forgot to change the sheets and the pillowcase. Small particles from the feather comforter were still sticking on the bed sheet. That was powerful enough to cause allergenic symptoms in Jane because she was highly allergic to the substance. She was the most willing researcher of all my patients. She agreed not to use the comforter for another week. Se went home and changed the sheets, pillowcases, vacuumed the carpet and cleaned all the dusty surfaces. That night she did not have any stomach pain or discomfort. She waited for three more nights and she still did not have any discomfort what so ever.

She walked into the office on the following day with a mile long smile. By this time she was a believer in NTT. She was ready to get the allergen out of her body. Now she was anxious to put NAET to work and see if it really would do what it said. She was treated for egg mix. It was easy for her to avoid since she never used them. After 30 hours (she had to stay away from egg and feather for 30 hours according to testing by NTT), she took out the feather comforter and used it. She slept soundly that night without any trace of previous discomfort.

CHEMICALS

(drinking water, tap water, chlorine, swimming pool water, detergents, fabric softener, soaps, cleaning products, shampoo, lipstick, cosmetics you or other family members use).

A 46-year-old woman severely reacted to Clorox bleach. An emotional allergy was discovered with this case. When she was a new bride at 19, she scrubbed and cleaned the kitchen sink. Her father-in-law walked in and praised her, saying what a good job she did, that he wasn't aware a sink could shine like that, since he had never seen it before. Her mother-in-law stood next to her with a deep hurt in her eyes. She responded, saying that she always kept the wash basin cleaner than that but he never bothered to notice it, even once. This made the daughter-in-law very unhappy. Ever since that time, she reacted to the smell or touch of any chemicals. When she was treated for the incident, she was able to use chemicals and detergents without any adverse reactions.

IS THIS MY CANDIDA?

    I have been a patient of Dr. Devi for three years. When I first started the allergy treatments, I was in pretty bad condition. My health deteriorated twelve years ago when I came down with chronic fatigue. I had constant sinus infections for years, and the antibiotics I took gave me candida. I suffered from severe systemic candida for years. I had frequent headaches, body pain, bladder infections, and a fever for over a year and a half. And my uterus was detaching and I had large cysts on my ovaries. I was exhausted all the time. I saw many doctors during the past 12 years and everyone of them diagnosed my condition as overgrowth of candida and yeast as my only problem.

    I went through various detox and took the mercury out of my teeth, tried to eat healthy at home, spent thousands of dollars and suffered the pain and agony everyday in spite of everything. I suffered from severe insomnia too. Doctors could offer only drugs, surgery, and exercise. But when you have to rest to get upstairs in your house, it is pretty hard to exercise.

    I tried everything that I knew to get well, including a healthy diet, rest, and acupuncture with Chinese herbal teas, at great expense. This helped some, but not permanently. Little did I know I was allergic to everything I was eating and drinking along with the environmental pollutions. Previous allergy testing only showed environmental allergies. I was 38-years-old and I thought my life was over. After I started treatment *with Dr. Devi my health has steadily improved. It took about three months of basic treatments, treating the chronic fatigue and ca*ndida after which I noticed a change. When I was treated for minerals the cysts on my ovaries disap*peared and my uterus re-attached.*

A sonogram and examination confirmed and showed everything as normal once again. I still receive treatments once in a while for ocassional new allergy. But I have a life again. All my infections are long gone and headaches are rare. I exercise and I know I will live a long life in health and with energy.

Janet Johnson

Riverside, CA

HORMONES (female and male hormones).

OTHER HORMONES (thyroid hormones, pituitary hormone)

IMMUNIZATIONS AND VACCINATIONS (DPT, POLIO, MMR, small pox, chicken pox, influenza, and hepatitis), you received or your parent received before you were born.

A 42-year-old man suffered from chronic irritable bowel syndrome, insomnia, and nervousness. He was unable to organize his belongings, bills, or any projects he needed to complete at work and could only hold a job for a few months at a time before he had to let go. After all of his basic allergies were treated, he was evaluated and tested through NTT. His problem was traced to the polio vaccine that he had received as an infant. He was immediately treated for the polio vaccine. He had severe abdominal pains and watery stools for two weeks following the initial NAET treatment. During this time, he had to repeat the treatment for polio vaccine six times. When he finally completed the treatments, he said good-bye to his irritable bowel syndrome, insomnia, and nervousness. He has a job with a large software company, which he has held for over a year now!

PRESCRIPTION DRUGS Any drugs given in infancy, during childhood or taken by the mother during pregnancy (antibiotics, cortisone, sedatives, laxatives, recreational drugs).

INSECT MIX (bee stings, spider bites, cockroach, etc.). Any insect bites in infancy or childhood.

PERFUME MIX (room deodorizers, soaps, flowers, perfumes, after-shave, etc.).

Two-year-old Serena was brought to us for a strange problem. Every day she woke up crying around 7:00 a.m. and continued to cry until 10:00 a.m. This became a routine in the house. She was seen by a pediatrician, an internist, and a homeopath without any results. When she was evaluated in my office, she was found to be allergic to many things. She was put on a regular NAET program. As soon as she was treated for coffee, caffeine, chocolate, she began crying, according to her mother, the cry sounded just like the usual morning cry. She failed coffee thrice. Every time she failed, she cried. She was treated three times every ten minutes. Finally she passed coffee mix and her crying stopped. The next morning her father went to the coffee shop to have his morning coffee. There was no coffee brewing in the house that morning and she didn't wake up crying.

The smell of coffee brewing caused her three-hour daily cry every morning.

COLORING BOOKS (books with colored illustrations)
Five-year-old Wes began to get very hyper every time he touched his coloring books. He would throw the crayons all over the room and tear pages out of the books. He refused to obey the parents or teachers. He started fights with his classmates. He was in constant motion during the class, jumping, climbing, running in the class like a four legged animal, he distracted every one around him. He couldn't sit still even for two minutes. With pressure from the school administration, he was placed on Ritalin to calm his brain. But, he was highly allergic to it. He was referred to us by his teacher for treatment of his allergy to Ritalin. He was also successfully treated for all the foods and environmental agents. He was found to be allergic to food colors, coloring books, crayons, and printed books with illustrations. After being treated for all these items he became quite normal when using them.

PESTICIDES (Malathion, termite control items, regular pesticides).
Sam, eleven-years-old, was brought to our office with a unique complaint. He became very hyper and suffered from restless leg syndrome only when he was in his bedroom. Through NTT, it was discovered that he was being exposed to some form of chemical spray. When I questioned his mother, she remembered that she periodically used ant spray in his room. After he was treated for pesticides, his hyperactivity and restless leg syndrome diminished. He became much calmer in his room.

RADIATION (computer, television, microwave, X-ray, sun):
A 33-year-old male, who worked for a software computer company complained of feeling irritable, restless, depressed, insecure, and angry. He could not focus on his work and had low self-

cure, and angry. He could not focus on his work and had low self-esteem. He was given medication for his symptoms, but the drugs made him sleepy and he was not able to do his work. By the time he arrived at the clinic, he was despondent. Through NTT, it was found that the keyboard material (plastic), computer monitors, carpets and formaldehyde caused his problem. After he was treated for the basic ten, plastics, chemicals, computer radiation and keyboard, he was able to function in his job without any of the symptoms that had been hindering him.

MOLD MIX

Many children and adults are affected by molds and fungus. Many people get respiratory problems from molds. Mold has also caused brain fatigue and brain fog in many people. After treating for mold and fungus, usually, affected people get relief from their symptoms.

Michel, 18-years-old suffered from ADHD symptoms all her life. She was on prescription medication for a number of years, which apparently helped her to keep her symptoms somewhat under control. She was able to go through school with the help of medication even though, she had repeated ups and downs along the way. She was also on a candida and yeast free diet. Going to college or finding a job was impossible. She was ready to give up because she was reacting to everything she ate or touched. She had lost weight, couldn't sleep, was shaky and hyper all the time. Her parents were concerned about her health and the fact that she had no friends or interaction with others. She always complained of restless leg syndrome and a sensation of something crawling all over, especially inside her head. She complained of severe brain fog and stabbing sharp pains in her brain intermittently through the day. Sitting in a hot tub with Epsom salt gave her some relief. She was examined and treated by various noted specialists throughout the country without giving her any relief. By the time she discovered NAET, it was difficult for her to go through the day

MY WHEAT ALLERGY!

I was very allergic to wheat. If I ate a touch of wheat in any form, I would suffer from panic attacks, severe mood swings, insomnia, abdominal cramps and diarrhea for next three weeks. I read all the labels carefully before I ate or bought anything from the market. I was so afraid of getting another attack. I didn't have a life. I couldn't go out with anyone for fear of getting sick. I lived alone. My life was getting pretty dry. A friend told me about NAET and Dr. Devi. I didn't waste another moment. Fortunately Dr. Devi's office was close to my home. I began NAET right away. After the B complex treatment, I was able to eat bread made with wheat. I had many food and chemical allergies. After the wheat treatment I didn't stop NAET. I was anxious to have a life that I was denied all these 37 years of my life. I have treated over 100 treatments so far. I am very happy to say that I have a life now. I can eat anything I want to, I can wear anything I like to (perfume, clothes, cosmetics, jewelry, etc), and I can go anywhere I like to. I can't thank Dr. Devi and NAET enough for giving me this chance to enjoy my life!

Sharon John, Orange, CA

CINNAMON- CAUSED MY PANIC ATTACKS

I suffered from nervousness, hyper-irritability, restlessness, and frequent panic attacks for two months. I couldn't continue to work due to nervousness. I felt a butterfly sensation in my stomach all the time. When I took my vacation (I had been accumulating vacation days for the past years for an overseas trip), I secretly saw a therapist. I was afraid to let anyone know about my illness thinking they might consider me for mentally ill. My job was very important. I couldn't afford to carry a label like that. I frantically searched everywhere for an answer. Then I read about NAET on the internet. Luckily Dr. Devi's office was near my home. She examined me and tested my arm strength at several times silently for about two minutes. Then she looked at me and asked me what kind of spice was I eating daily for the last two months. She said that was the culprit causing me to be nervous, paranoid, and irritable. I let out a deep sigh of relief. She tracked it down to the cinnamon that I was eating in the cereal every morning. She immediately treated me for cinnamon. Praise the Lord! Next morning I was free of my symptoms. I am back to myself again!

Thank you Dr. Devi for discovering NAET.
John Almirah, CA

without assistance even for her daily chores. After many NEAT treatments (40-50 groups of basics allergens), she began to respond positively to the NAET treatments. After the allergy treatments for yeast, candida and mold, her body was able to eliminate them naturally. She doesn't exhibit any of her previous symptoms any more, and her blood tests are clear for candida and yeast.

PARASITE MIX (pin worm, tape worm, hook worm, fish parasites, amoeba, giardia, and protozoa).

Many people host various parasites in the body. They find their way into our body via uncooked vegetables, meats, fish and unwashed fruits. Once when they get in they multiply rapidly and find their way into the blood stream. Parasite infestation can cause various health disorders in the body, including upper respiratory infections, asthma, brain fatigue, brain fog, fibromyalgia, insomnia, general itching, abdominal bloating, pain in the abdomen, sinusitis, diarrhea, anal itching, hyperactivity, irritability, mood swings, and unexplained weight gain (does not lose weight with low calorie food intake, exercise and any other weight control herbs and medications).

INHALANTS (pollens, weeds, grasses, flowers, wood mix, room air, outside air, smog, and polluted air from nearby factories).

ALLERGY TO B COMPLEX AND SUGAR

Dear Dr. Devi,

We were at your clinic for two weeks, two treatments a day, and I had no choice but to become an advocate of NAET. Alex is so thrilled to be able to eat cheese, catsup, and drink milk without her stomach blowing up like a balloon, and be able to eliminate two to three times a day instead of once a week, painfully. But, more than that, once you treated her for the chemicals that her parents were using before her gestation period, we saw a transformation before our very eyes. The trip home in the motor home was a whole new experience, so quiet and peaceful. No fights with her sister or temper tantrums. She looked at books, watched her favorite movies and even took a nap! It seemed too good to be true.

She has had several days in school now and they think that they have a new Alex in school. They are highly curious about what type of treatment could possibly make this kind of transformation in a child

Alex has never known any other way to express herself except in anger and fits of crying and tantrums. Its so wonderful to watch her try some of the same antics when she wants things her own way, and see the smile she has on her face when she realizes it doesn't feel right anymore. I can tease her out of her old habits now. I have never seen her positive side in such full bloom. We have also had to train ourselves to be more positive and to display our pleasure with her in her new found excitement.

"Grandma, I didn't cause any trouble at school today."

Dr. Devi, I feel as if there is hope for Alexandria in the school systems, in interpersonal relationships, and in life. I'm sure you will see us again as soon as possible to follow up on the additional treatments that time didn't allow. But, for now I thank you from the bottom of my heart! This is the most amazing, exciting experience I have had in my lifetime. We all benefited from your treatments, but Alexandria being the most crucial and in the most crisis benefited the most!

Sincerely yours,
Daisy L. Costa,
CALIFORNIA

TISSUES AND SECRETIONS (DNA, RNA, brain tissue, hypothalamus, liver, blood, saliva, urine).

PERSON TO PERSON ALLERGY Allergies to people, animals and pets (mother, father, caretakers, cats, and dogs).

EMOTIONAL ALLERGIES (fear, fright, frustration, anger, low self-esteem, rejection, etc., person to person allergies, like allergy to the mother, father, siblings).

Emotional allergies play a big role in ADD and ADHD children and adults. It is very important that patients and doctors should pay enough attention in this matter.

A six-year-old male child was brought to our office because he was hyperactive. His mother also said that he was very destructive in the house, breaking and throwing things and hurting his siblings. He fought with his older siblings all the time. He hurt his younger sister and made her cry. The mother was afraid to leave him alone with his siblings even for a few minutes.

He appeared very restless when his mother brought him into our office. He paced around the room without stopping for a moment. His mother kept telling him to calm down. He acted as if he did not hear her, but he responded fairly well to the office staff. When he was with one of the staff, he was calm and responded to her questions. He was able to tell his name, and he helped her put a puzzle together. The moment his mother walked into the room, his behavior changed dramatically. One of his neighbors, who had other children of the same age, told us that he behaved very normally whenever he went to play with her children in her house. His mother thought that probably the cats and dogs in their house could be the culprit for this strange behavior. He was very allergic to sugar and trace minerals.

He was treated for the food items, he still behaved the same. His older brother blamed the parents for giving him all the special attention. He was found to be allergic to his mother, father and other siblings. When he was treated for his family members, his behavior became normal. Two years later, he is a very happy loving and smart boy who doesn't get into too much mischief.

Say Good-bye to ADD and ADHD

CHAPTER TWELVE

NUTRITION CORNER

12

NUTRITION CORNER

Vitamins and trace minerals are essential to life. They contribute to good health by regulating the metabolism and assisting the biochemical processes that release energy from the foods and drinks we consume. Vitamins and trace minerals are micronutrients, and the body needs them in small amounts. The lack of these essential elements even though they are needed in minute amounts can create various impairments and tissue damage in the body. Water, carbohydrates, fats, proteins and bulk minerals like calcium, magnesium, sodium, potassium and phosphorus are considered to be macronutrients, taken into the body via regular food. They are needed in larger amounts. Both macro- and micronutrients are not only necessary to produce energy for our daily body functions, but also for growth and development of the body and mind.

Using macronutrients (food & drinks) and micronutrients (vitamins and trace minerals), the body creates some essential chemicals called enzymes and hormones. These are the foundation of human bodily functions. Enzymes are the catalysts, or simple activators, in the chemical reactions that are continually taking place in the body. Without the appropriate vitamins and trace minerals, the production and function of the enzymes will be incomplete. Prolonged deficiency of these vitamins and minerals can produce immature or incomplete enzyme production, protein synthesis, cell mutation, immature RNA, DNA synthesis, etc., which can mimic various organic diseases in the body.

Deficiency of vitamins and other essentials in the body can be due to poor intake and absorption. Nutritional imbalances can mainly be attributed to allergies.

Many ADHD children and adults have nutritional deficiencies due to poor eating habits and will benefit from nutritional supplements and megavitamin therapy. Others may have nutritional deficiencies due to food allergies and will not show any improvements on vitamin therapy.

All ADHD people should be tested for possible allergies before. If they are found to be allergic, they should be treated for the allergies before they are supplemented with vitamin and minerals.

Apart from allergies, one needs to know a few things about taking vitamins and minerals. Of the major vitamins, vitamin C and B complex vitamins are water-soluble while vitamins A, D, E, and K are fat-soluble. It is believed that water-soluble vitamins must be taken into the body daily, as they cannot be stored and are excreted within one to four days, (although our clinical experience has proven otherwise).

When a patient is allergic to vitamin B complex, in many cases she or he cannot digest grains, resulting in B complex deficiencies. When one gets treated for allergies via NAET, she/he can eat grains, without any ill effect and will begin to assimilate Bcomplex vitamins. In some cases through NTT I have found B complex deficiency amounting to fifteen to twenty thousand times the normal daily-recommended allowances. After supplementing with large amounts of B complex for a few weeks (20 – 30 times of RDA amount per day for a week or so), the deficiency was eliminated.

Over and over in hundreds of patients, after supplementing for weeks, we have been able to remove their vitamin B complex deficiency symptoms completely. This proves that vitamin B complex is stored in the body. We have received similar results with vitamin C. But more research is needed on a larger number of patients to verify these findings.

Fat-soluble vitamins are stored for longer periods of time in the body's fatty tissue and the liver. When you are allergic to fat soluble vitamins, you begin to store them in unwanted places of the body. Some of the abnormal vitamin storage can be seen as lipomas, warts, skin tags, benign tumors inside or outside the body, etc.

Taking vitamins and minerals in their proper balance is important for the correct functioning of all vitamins. Excess consumption of an isolated vitamin or mineral can produce unpleasant symptoms of that particular nutrient. High doses of one element can also cause depletion of other nutrients in the body, leading to other problems. Most of these vitamins work synergistically, complementing and/or strengthening each other's function.

Vitamins and minerals should be taken with meals unless specified otherwise. Oil-soluble vitamins should be taken before meals, and water-soluble vitamins should be taken between or after meals. But when you are taking megadoses of any of these, they should always be taken with or after meals. Vitamins and minerals, as nutritional supplements taken with meals, will supply the missing nutrients in our daily diets.

Synthetic vitamins are produced in a laboratory from isolated chemicals with quality similar to natural vitamins. Although there are no major chemical differences between a vitamin found in food and one created in a laboratory, natural supplements do not contain other unnatural ingredients. Supplements that are not labeled natural may include coal tars, artificial coloring, preservatives, sugars, and starches, as well as other additives. Vitamins labeled natural may contain vitamins that have not been extracted from a natural food source.

There are various books available on nutrition today that are helpful in understanding vitamins and their assimilative processes. If you are interested in learning more about nutrition, there are titles listed in the bibliography section, at the end of this book.

VITAMIN A

Clinical studies have proven vitamin A and beta-carotene to be very powerful immune-stimulants and protective agents.

Vitamin A is necessary for proper vision and in preventing night blindness, skin disorders, and acne. It protects the body against colds, influenza and other infections. It enhances immunity, helps heal ulcers and wounds and maintains the epithelial cell tissue. It is necessary for the growth of bones and teeth.

Vitamin A works best with B complex, vitamin D, vitamin E, calcium, phosphorus and zinc. Zinc is needed to get vitamin A out of the liver, where it is usually stored. Large doses of vitamin A should be taken only under proper supervision, because it can accumulate in the body and become toxic.

Many teenagers with an allergy to vitamin A have acne, blemishes and other skin problems. People with allergy to vitamin A develop skin tags, and warts, and pimples around the neck, arms, etc. It is, also, one of the causes of premenstrual syndrome. When they get treated and properly supplemented with vitamin A, the skin clears up and PMS problems become less severe.

VITAMIN D

Vitamin D is often called the sunshine vitamin. It is a fat-soluble vitamin, acquired through sunlight or food sources. Vitamin D is absorbed from foods, through the intestinal wall, after they are ingested. Smog reduces the vitamin D producing rays of the sun. Dark-skinned people and sun-tanned people do not absorb vitamin D from the sun. Vitamin D helps the utilization of calcium and phosphorus in the human body. When there is an allergy to vitamin D, the vitamin is not absorbed into the body through foods, or from the sun. People with an allergy to vitamin D can exhibit deficiency syndromes: rickets, severe tooth decay, softening of teeth and bones, osteomalacia, senile osteoporosis, sores on the skin, blisters on the skin while walking in the sun, severe sunburns when exposed to the sun, etc. Sometimes allergic persons can show toxic symptoms if they take vitamin D without clearing its allergy. These symptoms include mental confusion, unusual thirst, sore eyes, itching skin, vomiting, diarrhea, urinary urgency, calcium deposits in the blood vessels and bones, restlessness in the sun, and inability to bear heat. Vitamin D works best with vitamin A, vitamin C, choline, calcium, and phosphorus.

When an allergy to vitamin D is treated by NAET, the deficiency or toxic symptoms can be eliminated and gradually with the proper supplementation, normal health can be restored.

VITAMIN E

Vitamin E is an antioxidant. The body needs zinc in order to maintain the proper levels of vitamin E in the blood. Vitamin E is a fat-soluble vitamin and is stored in the liver, fatty tissues, heart, muscles, testes, uterus, blood, adrenal glands and pituitary glands. Vitamin E is excreted in the feces if too much is taken.

VITAMIN K

Vitamin K is needed for blood clotting and bone formation. Vitamin K is necessary to convert glucose into glycogen for storage in the liver. Vitamin K is a fat-soluble vitamin, very essential to the formation of prothrombin, a blood-clotting material. It helps in the blood-clotting mechanism, prevents hemorrhages (nosebleeds and intestinal bleeding) and helps reduce excessive menstrual flow.

An allergy to vitamin K can produce deficiency syndromes such as prolonged bleeding time, intestinal diseases like sprue, etc., and colitis.

VITAMIN B

Approximately 15 vitamins make up the B complex family. Each one of them has unique, very important functions in the body. If the body does not absorb and utilize any or all of the B-vitamins, various health problems can result. B complex vitamins are very essential for emotional, physical and physiological well being of the human body. It is a nerve food, so it is necessary for the proper growth and maintenance of the nervous system and brain function. It also keeps the nerves well fed so that nerves are kept calm and the ADHD person can maintain a good mental attitude.

B-vitamins are seen in almost all foods we eat. Cooking and heating destroy some of them, others are not destroyed by processing or preparation. People who are allergic to B-vitamins can get mild to severe reactions just by eating the foods alone. If they are supplemented with vitamin B complex, without being aware of the allergies, such people can get exaggerated reactions. One has to be very cautious when taking B complex, commonly called stress vitamins.

Dr. Carlton Frederic, in his book, "Psychonutrition," tried to point out that nutritional deficiencies are the causes of most of the mental irritations such as extreme anger, severe mod swings, bipolar diseases, schizophrenic disorders, frontal lobe disorders, anxiety disorders, attention deficit disorders, hyperactivity disorders, various neurological disorders, mental sicknesses including mild to moderate to severe psychiatric disorders. He tried to prove his theory by giving large doses of vitamin B complex, especially B-12, to some of the psychiatric patients. Fifty percent of the patients got better, were cured of their mental sickness and went back to live normal lives. But another 50 percent made no progress or got worse. He couldn't explain why the other 50% got worse. His theory was ridiculed and his treatment protocol with mega B complex vitamin therapy for mental disorders was thown out by the want of proof. He did not think in the direction of allergies. When I discovered the allergic connection, I tried to contact him to let him know that his theory was absolutely right and I had proof to support his theory. Unfortunately, I was a year late to reach him...he had passed away a year before my discovery of NAET.

A few minerals are extremely essential for our daily functions. While some metals and trace minerals are mentioned here, for more information on other minerals, please refer to the appropriate references in the bibliography.

CALCIUM

Calcium is one of the essential minerals in the body. Calcium works with phosphorus, magnesium, iron, vitamins A, C and D. Calcium helps to maintain strong bones and healthy teeth. It regulates the heart functions and helps to relax the nerves and muscles. It induces relaxation and sleep.

Deficiencies in calcium result in rickets, osteomalacia, osteoporosis, hyperactivity, restlessness, inability to relax, general-

Deficiencies in calcium result in rickets, osteomalacia, osteoporosis, hyperactivity, restlessness, inability to relax, generalized aches and pains, joint pains, formation of bone spurs, backaches, PMS, cramps in the legs and heavy menstrual flow.

Many ADHD children and adults respond well to calcium supplementation. Often ADHD people suffer from abdominal pains, dysentery, insomnia, skin problems, nervousness, dyslexia, canker sores, post-nasal drip, hyperactivity, obesity, and joint disorders. They all respond well to calcium supplementation after allergy elimination. When people are on cortisone treatment, they need to take more calcium.

IRON

Iron deficiency results in anemia. People with allergy to iron do not absorb iron from food. They suffer from iron deficiency anemia, even though they take iron supplements. A person with iron allergy can get various problems from iron supplementation or eating iron-containing foods.

COBALT

Cobalt is essential for red blood cells, since it is part of vitamin B-12. Deficiency results in B-12 anemia.

COPPER

Copper is required to convert the body's iron into hemoglobin. Combined with the amino acid thyroxin, it helps to produce the pigment factor for hair and skin. It is essential for utilization of vitamin C. Deficiency results in anemia and edema. Toxicity symptoms are insomnia, hair loss, irregular menses and depression.

FLUORIDE

Sodium fluoride is added to drinking water. Calcium fluoride is seen in natural food sources. Fluorine decreases chances of dental carries, (too much can discolor teeth). It also strengthens the bones. Deficiency leads to tooth decay. Toxicity or allergy symptoms include dizziness, nausea, poor appetite, skin rashes, itching, yeast infections, mental confusion, muscle spasms, mental fogginess and arthritis. Treatment for fluoride will eliminate possible allergies.

IODINE

Two thirds of the body's iodine is in the body's thyroid gland. Since the thyroid gland controls metabolism, and iodine influences the thyroid, an under supply of this mineral can result in weight gain, general fatigue and slow mental reaction. Iodine helps to keep the body thin, promotes growth, gives more energy, improves mental alertness, and promotes the growth of hair, nails and teeth.

A deficiency in iodine can cause overweight, hyperthyroidism, goiters and lack of energy. Among its food sources are kelp, seafood, iodized salt, vegetables grown in iodine-rich soil and onion.

MAGNESIUM

This is one of the important minerals to help with irritability and hyperactivity. Magnesium is necessary for the metabolism of calcium, vitamin C, phosphorus, sodium, potassium and vitamin A. It is essential for the normal functioning of nerves and muscles. It also helps convert blood sugar into energy. It works as a natural tranquilizer, laxative and diuretic. Diuretics deplete magnesium. Alcoholics and asthmatics are deficient in magnesium.

MANGANESE

Manganese helps to activate digestive enzymes in the body. It is important in the formation of thyroxin, the principal hormone of the thyroid gland. It is necessary for the proper digestion and utilization of food. Manganese is important in reproduction and the normal functioning of the central nervous system. It helps to eliminate fatigue, improves memory, reduces nervous irritability and relaxes the mind. A deficiency may result in recurrent attacks of dizziness and poor memory.

MOLYBDENUM

Molybdenum helps in carbohydrate and fat metabolism. It is a vital part of the enzyme responsible for iron utilization.

PHOSPHORUS

Phosphorus is involved in virtually all-physiological chemical reactions in the body. It is necessary for normal bone and teeth formation. It is important for heart regularity, and is essential for normal kidney function. It provides energy and vigor by helping in the fat and carbohydrate metabolism. It promotes growth and repairs in the body. It is essential for healthy gums and teeth. Vitamin D and calcium are essential for its proper functioning.

POTASSIUM

Potassium works with sodium to regulate the body's water balance and to regulate the heart rhythm. It helps in clear thinking by sending oxygen to the brain. A deficiency in potassium results in edema, hypoglycemia, nervous irritability, and muscle weakness.

SELENIUM

Selenium is an antioxidant. It works with vitamin E, slowing down the aging process. It prevents hardening of tissues and helps to retain youthful appearance. Selenium is also known to alleviate hot flashes and menopausal distress. It prevents dandruff. Some researchers have found selenium to neutralize certain carcinogens and provide protection from some cancers.

SODIUM

Sodium is essential for normal growth and normal body functioning. It works with potassium to maintain the sodium-potassium pump in the body. Potassium is found inside the cells and sodium is found outside.

SULFUR

Sulfur is essential for healthy hair, skin and nails. It helps maintain the oxygen balance necessary for proper brain function. It works with B-complex vitamins for basic body metabolism. It is a part of tissue building amino acid. It tones up the skin and makes the hair lustrous and helps fight bacterial infection.

VANADIUM

Vanadium prevents heart attacks. It inhibits the formation of cholesterol in blood vessels.

ZINC

Zinc is essential to form certain enzymes and hormones in the body. It is very necessary for protein synthesis. It is important for blood stability and in maintaining the body's acid-alkaline balance. It is important in the development of reproductive organs and helps to normalize the prostate glands in males. It helps in treatment of mental disorders and speeds up healing of wounds and cuts on the body. Zinc helps with the growth of fingernails and eliminates cholesterol deposits in the blood vessels.

TRACE MINERALS

Even though trace minerals are needed in our body, they are seen in trace amounts only. The researchers do not know definite functions of the trace minerals but deficiencies can definitely contribute toward health problems.

AMINO ACIDS

All proteins are made up of amino acids. They are the building blocks of protein. There are 22 different types of amino acids. Some can be made in the body and are called non-essential amino acids. Eight are not produced in the body and are known as essential amino acids. These essential amino acids that have to be absorbed from food are lysine, methionine, leucine, threonine, valine, tryptophan, isoleucine and phenylalanine. Children also need histidine and arginine.

LECITHIN

Every living cell in the human body needs lecithin. Cell membranes, which regulate which nutrients may leave or enter the cell, are largely composed of lecithin. Cell membranes would harden without lecithin. Its structure protects the cells from damage by oxidation. The protective sheaths surrounding the brain are composed of lecithin, and the muscles and nerve cells also contain this essential fatty substance. Lecithin is composed of choline, inositol, and linoleic acids. It acts as an emulsifying agent.

It helps prevent arteriosclerosis, protects against cardiovascular disease, increases brain function, and promotes energy. It promotes better digestion of fats and helps disperse cholesterol in water and removes it from the body. The vital organs and arteries are protected from fatty build-up with the inclusion of lecithin in the diet. Most lecithin is derived from soybean, eggs, brewer's yeast, grains, legumes, fish, and wheat germ.

The body needs all of the essential vitamins and minerals in proper proportion for its normal function. If there is any deficiency of the vitamins, minerals, trace minerals, or amino acids, it can be seen as some functional disorder or other problem. If it can be found in time and treated or supplemented with appropriate amounts, many unnecessary discomforts can be avoided.

CHAPTER THIRTEEN

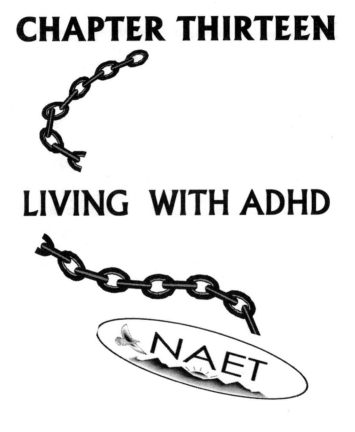

LIVING WITH ADHD

13

LIVING WITH ADHD

AS A CHILD WITH ADD OR ADHD

I f children are too small to understand that they are hyperactive or have ADHD, parents can help them in many ways as you will see on the following pages. If the diagnosis is made at school age, the child should be told about his/her health disorder. Parent(s) should be the best person(s) to make the child understand about his/her unique health condition. If the parent (either one or both together), cannot talk to the child without getting too emotional, or upset, his/her doctor or counselor can explain to him/her. This is for the child's sake to avoid unnecessary embarrassment.

Even though ADHD is recognized as an imbalance in the brain chemistry, the common lay public still view ADHD children and adults as weird, abnormal and/or eccentric people. They are being mistreated by their siblings, relatives, classmates, playmates, and other children from the neighborhood by name calling and teasing, etc. So the ADD child should be warned and prepared to face the real world. This should be done gently by the parents. If it comes from the parents it is less traumatic for the child. Once the child understands his/her unique condition, it would become easier to explain his/her behaviors calmly to others. If other children knew why the child with ADHD acted differently, they would be less likely to make fun of the child or his/her weaknesses. It is everyone's responsiblity, the teacher, counselor, principal, coach, as well as the parents to use the appropriate medical terminology to explain the child's health problem to the other children he/she comes in contact with so they will not tease or annoy the child and leave him/her alone. Not only that, if the need arises, other children should be willing and ready to help the child with any of his difficult chores. So, an ADHD child's future depends on how the family (parents) presents his/her problem to the world.

SELF-ESTEEM

Self-esteem plays a major role in the positive development of the child and his/her relationship with his/her siblings, family, friends and school. Every one should give the child enough attention to maintain his/her self-esteem. The ADHD child should be taught to think positively about everything in his/her life. This comes only by constant training and coaching from a very young age since one of the problems ADHD children and adults face is negative thinking. Parents should begin the necessary training from a very young age.

LEARNING DIFFICULTIES

Usually, ADHD children suffer from learning disabilities. Parents should spend extra time to take care of the child's tutoring needs from a young age. If the parents cannot tutor him/her for some reason, a special tutor should be appointed to give the child extra help in his/her weak subjects. With extra coaching most children will be able to do well in school. Getting good grades in school helps to develop a good self-image. Usually, ADHD people are very intelligent. Due to the irritability of the brain, they cannot utilize their intelligence. Irritability may be due to allergies to food and environmental factors. Their brain will begin to work and focus appropriately soon after the allergy is eliminated with NAET.

OUT-DOOR ACTIVITIES

ADHD children should be included and encouraged in all normal activities of the school, like playing sports, games, picnics, field trips, neighborhood cleaning, feeding the poor in the community, church and/or religious group activities, etc. Other children should be made to understand his/her condition and weakness, so that others won't embarrass or put the child down if he/she is slow or disorganized.

HOME SCHOOLING

Home schooling is another option available to ADHD children. It might hinder social development and interaction slightly by not going to school, especially if parents do not take enough steps to get them involved in supervised extracurricular activities such as sports, karate, music classes, boy scouts, or community volunteer programs, etc. Home schooling can turn out to be a good program for ADHD children when the extra curricular activies are added. Implementing and managing a regular activity schedule takes time, patience, and tireless effort on the parent's part. But it is worth it. Home schooling will allow an ADHD child to learn at his/her own pace without becoming the victim of the scrutiny of other less considerate classmates and some teachers. This also can help the child to develop and maintain his/her self-worth and self-esteem so that he/she can eventually grow up into a normal, efficient, and responsible adult.

NAET TREATMENTS

An ADHD child should be tested and treated for all basic allergies as soon as possible. He/she should be taught how to self-test for his/her allergies. He /she should make a point to test everything before using them. Any item tested as allergic, should be avoided until he/she gets treated with NAET.

After the NAET allergy treatments, the offending allergen should not cause problems. But even after the successful NAET treatment, always remember to test for allergy to every item, including the kind you have been treated for in the past, before you use them. You may have been treated for an apple six months ago, but the new apple may have something else on it, like a new pesticide, chemical spray, grown in a new soil, etc., and anything new on it can trigger a reaction in the ADHD child.

NUTRITION

After treating for the NAET basics, proper care should be taken to maintain a well balanced diet from the non-allergic food groups. The day can be started with the brain nectar tonic. ADD and ADHD children and adults deplete B complex vitamins and trace minerals very fast. These vitamins should be replaced appropriately in their daily diets. They should be encouraged to drink plenty of water (6-8 glasses daily).

EXERCISE

Various brain balancing exercises and activities are described in Chapter 9. Children should make a regular habit of implementing some of those exercises every day to maintain a stable mind.

SELF AWARENESS

The child should be educated and trained to pay attention to the presence of any commonly seen symptoms of ADHD. Any new allergen is capable of reproducing the old physical symptoms or creating a new symptom in a sensitive person. If the child is aware of this and exhibits any of these symptoms unexpectedly (when in contact with a new allergen in a new place), the child will not panic and would be able to pay more attention and make a conscious effort to prevent them in front of strangers. Self-instruction, where a child is mentally trained to remind himself/herself is an effective form of mental exercise that can help the child to act and react appropriately in social situations, and can also develop organizational skills. It is okay to take an appropriate drug prescribed by your physician in uncontrollable situations. Have your physician prescribe a non-allergic medication. If the child is allergic to the medication, he/she should be treated for the allergy to the medicine with NAET. The child doesn't have to take the medication regularly after sufficient NAET treatments have been received. But always make a point to have the prescription medication available for any emergency that occurs without warning.

AS A PARENT OF AN ADHD CHILD

As a parent, care of the ADHD child should begin before anyone else detects your child's abnormality. There are many books written on normal growth and development of children. All parents should begin reading these books when they plan to have a child, and read through these educational materials during pregnancy, or before the child is born. Watch the child closely when he/she is growing up. Pay attention to his /her emotional and physical needs wisely. It is advisable to take your infant to a NAET practitioner and get his/her allergies tested and treated if needed before they become a problem. NAET can be used as a good preventive measure.

Parents should make enough time to spend with the child from infancy, by touching, cuddling, caressing, talking to them and visiting places and meeting people. Parents should tell the child repeatedly how much they love him/her and how important he/she is in their lives. The child should be made to feel worthy from infancy by the action of the parents. If the infant seems to be restless, hyper, suffers from insomnia, repeated crying spells, temper tantrums, use all the mind calming techniques in Chapter 9 from the very beginning. Whenever such uncomfortable symptoms are exhibited, it is due to some irritation in the body. So, hold the child and massage the vertex of the head (top of the head) for a few minutes. This reduces the irritability temporarily. If parents learn to pay enough attention to the child's every day changes, the problem can be caught at an early age and the treatment can be provided immediately, sparing them from unnecessary anxious moments in the future.

If the parents did not discover the abnormalities in infancy, they do not have to feel guilty or less efficient. When ever the problem is discovered in your child, begin working with these methods immediately and results will happen before you know it.

ADHD diagnosis of a child affects the entire family. Usually most parents go into a denial stage initially. But it shouldn't last too long. An ADHD child brings tremendous inconvenience and re-adjustments in the parents' and other siblings' lives. But they all should learn to cooperate and help the child to grow up into a normal adult. Family members should be very patient with an ADHD child. It doesn't mean that parents shouldn't discipline the child. Take extra time to calmly explain all the rules of the family and what is expected and follow through. If you lay out the rules and never ask the child to follow them, or never check to see if he has followed them, children, even an ADHD child, will lose respect for the parent. Children watch you closely and if they think they can get away with something they will try every possible avenue. So it is for the parents to teach the child the right course of action from the beginning: putting toys away after play, washing hands after play, teaching him/her to appreciate things, to respect other's toys, books; teaching him/her to say 'thank you' and 'please', etc. Spend time with the child at bedtime telling him/her a bedtime story; giving him/her a gentle vertex massage. If there are more children in the family, consider reading bedtime stories as a group.

If there are siblings, make them take part in his/her daily activities, like washing him/her, dressing, feeding, etc. Siblings will feel very important and give them a sense of responsibility in rearing him/her and this will reduce your burden and solve the sibling rivalry. As the child grows up, parents should include him/her in everyday house chores, like cleaning the house, mowing the lawn, making breakfast, lunch and dinner, setting the dining table, etc. This gives them enough training and confidence, making them feel important in the family and that improves self-image. Improving family life with an ADD child takes understanding, patience, effort and love. Love conquers all obstacles in life. All the children (siblings) should be taught to share and care, love, and support each other from the beginning. With everyone's support and effort, an ADHD child should grow up as normal as any other child in a loving, caring, atmosphere.

AS A TEACHER OF AN ADHD CHILD

Some teachers have special training in handling difficult cases like ADHD. It is good for parents to find a teacher with special educational background. Usually teachers in pre-schools and other small classes are well trained to observe any imbalances in small children. If the teacher notices any symptoms of ADD or ADHD he/she should give special attention to the child to determine if whatever he/she is observing is true or not. He/she should meet with the child alone to evaluate the mental status and behavioral pattern of the child. He/she should document the child's behavior and inform the parents, school authorities, and the school psychologist about the findings. He/she should spend extra time to explain things to the child and help him/her to improve any weak areas. The teacher should pay special attention to introduce the child to rest of the class and to include him/her in all class activities.

A teacher should know her/his students and make learning fun, by making the presentation more interesting by using appropriate visual and auditory aids. ADHD childen cannot focus more than few minutes on any single task. By alternating and rotating the visual and auditory stimuli every few minutes the teacher will encourage the child to be attentive, focus, and learn. Try to bring out the best in the children. Avoid focusing on the child's weakness and avoid speaking negatively about the child to others. Most of these children have higher I.Qs., even though they may have behavioral problems and trouble focusing their attention on one thing. The teacher should be patient with the child. Care should be taken not to lose temper or tease him/her in front of other children. The teacher should not impose excessive punishments for minor things, or forget to reward the child when he/she does accomplish small tasks.

SEEKING PROFESSIONAL HELP

When behavior management enforced by parents and teachers turns ineffective, professional help from counselors and psychotherapists may be necessary to guide him/her properly. There are psychologists and therapists with special training and experience in specific areas of behavioral problems of children with different disorders. Their services often prove invaluable in controlling your child. Parents also could benefit from some counseling to cope with the situation.

MEDICATION

There are various reasons for someone to depend on medication. Some parents feel they have to keep their children medicated. In some severe cases, it may be necessary to keep them medicated to help them go through school, and other activities of life. In some cases, when both parents are working to find enough income to make ends meet, it may be very straining for parents to find the extra time to spend with the child. So keeping the child on medication reduces the stress and gets the work done. Some regular schools make it mandatory for the child to be on medication. Otherwise, the child is denied admission. Whatever the reason may be to give medication to your child, at least make sure that he/she is not allergic to it. Medication may be okay for a short term. Long term medication should be avoided. If the child gets his/her allergies eliminated through NAET, he/she may not require long term medication.

ADHD ADULTS

Whatever happens to ADD and ADHD children if they have never been treated either by medication, behavior modification or holistically? When the ADHD child is allowed to grow without any treatment, a few will outgrow it completely and become normal adults. A small percentage of the children outgrow ADHD, but turn their problem in another direction, getting asthma, migraines, and arthritis, etc. Some lucky ones get a break and discover NAET, like Dennis Wilber in the opening chapter. Others will never hear about NAET or will refuse to seek help saying they need scientific validation before they treat with NAET. Some might brush the idea off saying "it is too hard to follow the diet for 25 hours and there are too many treatments to take... no way, I can't do it. If I were a child I could have done it. But now, I will swallow my pills and see what happens."

No one knows the exact percentage of children and adolescents who continue to have ADHD as adults. It is estimated that about 40-50% of ADHD children will carry this disorder to adulthood. If the current estimate is right, 3 to 6 percent of the youth have ADHD so we might say 2 to 3 percent of adults have ADHD.

EVALUATING ADHD ADULTS

The procedure for evaluating and establishing the diagnosis for ADHD adults is the same as evaluating a child with ADHD. The classical ADHD signs, inattention, hyperactivity, impulsivity, and distractibility are seen in ADHD adults just the way they are seen in children with this disorder. The impact of ADHD on an adult might be the same as it is for children with ADHD. But it is reflected on an adult differently due to the fact that an adult's life is totally different with different demands and expectations. A child is under the care or supervision of a parent, guardian, teacher or care taker. An adult is expected to work, meet other demands of life, bring up a family, do community work, and meet social obligations within the community, family or friends. The impact of life can be overwhelming to an ADHD adult.

ADHD adults always find difficulty sitting still for a long time anywhere. So they would tend to be very active in their life. They will find jobs and lifestyles that requires them to be on the move all the time. They would be happier at a job that requires them to move around, drive, or go from place to place. If they have to continue on a job where they must sit for a long time, you will see them moving constantly in their seats, tapping their knees, swinging their legs, drumming with their toes, and snapping their fingers, etc.

Some of these people become obsessed with exercise, running, jogging or working out for hours in the gym. If they don't do that they feel restless and unsatisfied. Exercise will improve their circulation, help to eliminate toxins through sweat, urine and other secretory mechanism of the body. All the toxins produced in the body are burned out daily through exercise so that their body can be free from toxins for a while and they can do some productive work. Soon after exercise, they can think better.

Some people with ADHD are constant thinkers. They complain that they cannot stop thinking. Their minds wander a 1000 miles per minute and it can become difficult to turn their chain of thoughts off. They also have problems with insomnia because their mind continues to jump from thought to thought through the night. Handling jobs, relationships, marriage, family life, etc. becomes difficult for an ADHD adult.

ADHD adults talk incessantly without being aware of it. They keep talking without thinking, or without giving others a chance to talk. They interupt people during conversations, get into arguments without respecting others' ideas, and can talk inappropriately or make foolish remarks. Because of the above interpersonal difficulties, they have problems making and keeping friends.

Impulsivity is another trait of people with ADHD. They will buy anything on the spot without thinking or checking to see if they can afford it. They can get addicted easily to eating, drinking coffee, alcohol, drugs, collecting unwanted things, cluttering, gambling, stealing, cheating, and lying, etc.

ADHD people are poor drivers, they speed unnecessarily, change lanes without looking, take unnecessary risks, and have more accidents and traffic tickets than normal people. Absent mindedness (losing possessions like credit cards, driver's license, keys, sunglasses), and carelessness, etc., are symptoms of ADHD in a less severe form.

Organizing materials at work, or home is also a problem for ADHD person. They will fall in the group of procrastinators, always late getting up, late getting to work, and have difficulty keeping on a time schedule.

Most of the above symptoms are familiar to all of us, because we all have displayed some of these symptoms at one time or another. These symptoms are the reactions of certain irritations in the body, which could be caused by allergies. When we look around, we see variations of these symptoms displayed in many people among us. We do not consider all these people to be ADHD adults. Some display a few of these symptoms at one time whereas others display one or two of the symptoms ocassionally. But people with ADHD display most of these symptoms most of the time.

The symptoms of ADHD varies from person to person and range from mild, to moderate, or to severe. People with mild symptoms can function and lead a life as close to normal as possible. All others may face difficulties in varying degrees throughout their lives.

NAET is not just for ADD and ADHD children, but it It can help any ADHD person regardless of age. So an ADHD adult should find an NAET practitioner near him and begin NAET treatments as soon as possible so they too can "SAY GOOD-BYE to ADD and ADHD," and lead a productive life.

RESOURCES

RESOURCES

NAET
6714 Beach Blvd
Buena Park, CA 90621
(714) 523-8900
Website: naet.com
E-mail: naet@earthlink.net

NARF (Nambudripad's Research Foundation)
6714 Beach Blvd
Buena Park, CA 90621
(714) 523-0800
Website: naet.com
E-mail: naet@earthlink.net

Adult Support Network
Mary Jane Johnson
2620 Ivy Place
Toledo, OH 43613

Attention Deficit Resource Center
1344 Johnson Ferry Road, Suite 14
Marietta, GA 30068

Attention-Deficit Disorders Association (ADDA)
P.O. Box 972
Mentor, OH 44061

Association for Children and
Adults with Learning Disabilities
5156 Library Road
Pittsburgh, PA15234
(412) 341-8077

Orton Dyslexia Society
724 York Road
Baltimore, MD 21204
(301) 296-0232

Children with Attention
Deficit Disorders (C.H.A.D.D)
1859 North Pine Island Road, Suite 185
Plantation, FL 33322
(305) 384-6869

Newsletters
Adult News
2620 Ivy Place
Toledo, OH 43613

The Advisor
1344 Johnson Ferry Road, Suite 14
Marietta, GA 30068

Bibliography

BIBLIOGRAPHY

Abehsera, Michel, ed. *Healing Ourselves*. New York, 1973.

Austin, Mary. *Acupuncture Therapy*. New York, 1972.

Ali, Majid M.D. *The Canary and Chronic Fatigue*. New Jersey: Life Span Press, 1995.

American Medical Association Committee on Rating of Mental and Physical Impairments. *Guides to the Evaluation of Permanent Impairment*. N.P., 1971

Barkley, Russell A. Attention Deficit Hyperactivity Disorder: A Handbook for Diagnosis and Treatment. New York: Guildford Press, 1990.

Bender, David, and Bruno Leone. *The Environment, Opposing Viewpoints*. San Diego: Greenhaven Press, 1996.

Blum, Jeanne Elizabeth. *Woman Heal Thyself*. Boston: Charles E. Tuttle Co., Inc., 1995.

Brodal, A., M.D. *Neurological Anatomy in Relation to Clinical Medicine*. 2nd ed. New York.

Cerrat, Paul L., *"Does Diet Affect the Immune System?"* RN, Vol. 53, pp. 67-70 (June 1990).

Chaitow, Leon. *The Acupuncture Treatment of Pain*. New York: Thorsons Publishers Inc., 1984.

Chopra, Deepak, M.D. *Quantum Healing*. New York: Bantam Books, 1990.

Collins, Douglas, R. M.D. *Illustrated Diagnosis of Systematic Diseases*. Philadelphia, 1972.

Copeland, Edna D., and Valerie L. Love. Attention without Tension: A Teacher's Handbook on Attention Disorders (ADHD and ADD). Atlanta 3 C's of Childhood, 1992.

Daniels, Lucille, M.A. and Catherine Wothingham, Ph.D. *Muscle Testing Techniques of Manual Examination*. 3rd ed. Philadelphia, 1972

East Asian Medical Studies Society. *Fundamentals of Chinese Medicine*. Brookline: Paraadigm Publications, 1985.

Elliot, Frank, A., F.R.C.P. *Clinical Laboratory*. Philadelphia, 1959

Fazir, Claude A., M.D. *Parents Guide to Allergy in Children*. Garden City: Doubleday & Co. Inc. 1973.

Fulton, Shaton. *The Allergy Self Help Book*. Philadelphia: Rodale Books, 1983.

Fujihara, Ken, and Hays, Nancy. *Common Health Complaints*. Oriental Healing Arts Institute, 1982.

Graber, Stephen. *If Your Child is Hyperactive, Inattentive, Impulsive, Distractible....* New York:Villard Books, 1990.

Gach, Michael Reed. *Acuppressure's Potent Points*. New York: Bantam Books, 1990.

Golos, Natalie, and Frances. *Coping With Your Allergies*. New York: Simon and Schuster.

Goodheart, George, J. *Applied Kinesiology*. N.P., 1964

---. *Applied Kinesiology*, 1970 Research Manual, 8th ed. N.P., 1971

---. *Applied Kinesiology*, 1973 Research Manual. 9th ed. N.P., 1973

---. *Applied Kinesiology*, 1974 Research Manual. N.P., 1974

---.*Applied Kinesiology*, Workshop Manual. N.P., 1972.

Graziano, Joseph. *Footsteps to Better Health*, N.P., 1973

Gray, Henry, F.R.S. *Anatomy of the Human Body*. 27th, 34th, and 38th ed. Philadelphia, 1961.

Guyton, Arthur, C. *Textbook of Medical Physiology*. 2nd ed. Philadelphia, 1961.

Hansel, Tim. *When I Relax I Feel Guilty*. Colorado Springs: Chariot Victor Publishing, 1979.

Haldeman, Scott. *Modern Developments in the Principles and Practice of Chiropractic*. New York: Appleton-Century-Crofts, 1980.

Hepler, Opal, E., Ph.D., M.D. *Manual of Clinical Laboratory Methods*. 4th ed. Illinois, 1962.

Hsu, Hong-Yen, Ph.D. *Chinese Herb Medicine and Therapy*. Oriental Healing Arts Institute, 1982.

---. *Commonly Used Chinese Herb Formulas with Illustrations*. Oriental Healing Arts Institute, 1982.

---. *Natural Healing With Chinese Herbs*. Oriental Healing Arts Institute, 1982.

Heuns, Him-Che. *Handbook of Chinese Herbs and Formulae*. Vol V. Los Angeles, 1985.

Krohn, Jacqueline M.D., Francis A. Taylor, and Erla Mae Larson. *Allergy Relief and Prevention*. Vancouver: Hartley and Marks, 1996.

Krohn, Jacqueline, Francis A. Taylor, and Jinger Prosser. *Natural Detoxification.* Vancouver: Hartley Marks Publishers, 1996.

Kirschmann J. D. with L. J. Dunne. *Nutrition Almanac.* 2nd ed. McGraw Hill Book Co. Copyright 1984.

Lawson-Wood, Denis, F.A.C.A. and Joyce Lawson-Wood. *The Five Elements of Acupuncture and Chinese Massage.* 2nd ed. Northamptonshire, 1973.

Lyght, Charles E., M.D. and John M. Trapnell, M.D. eds. *The Merck Manual.* 11th ed. Rahway: Merck Research Laboratories, 1966.

Mindell, Earl. *Vitamin Bible.* New York: Warner Books, 1985.

Milne, Robert, M.D., Blake More, and Burton Goldberg. *An Alternative Medicine Definitive Guide to Headaches.* Tiburon, CA, 1997.

Moss, Louis, M.D. *Acupuncture and You.* New York, 1964.

Nambudripad, Devi S. *Say Good-bye to Illness*, Delta Publishing Co. Buena Park, CA, 1999

Nambudripad, Devi S. *Say Good-bye to ...series*, Delta Publishing Co., Buena Park, CA, 1999

Nambudripad, Devi S. *Living Pain Free,* Delta Publishing Co. , Buena Park, CA , 1997

Northrup, Christiane M.D. *Women's Bodies, Women's Wisdom.* New York: Bantam Books, 1998.

Palos, Stephan. *The Chinese Art of Healing.* New York, 1972.

Pearson, Durk, and Sandy Shaw. *The Life Extension Companion.* New York: Warner Books, 1984.

Kennington & Church. *Food Values of Portions Commonly Used.* J.B. Lippincott Company, 1998.

Pert, Candace B., Ph.D. *Molecules of Emotion.* New York: Scribner, 1997.

Pitchford, Paul. *Healing with Whole Foods.* Berkeley: North Atlantic Books, 1993.

Randolph, Theron, G.,M.D., and Ralph W. Moss, Ph.D. *An Alternative Approach to Allergies.* New York: Lippincott and Conwell, 1980.

Radetsky, Peter. *Allergic to the Twentieth Century.* Boston: Little, Brown and Co., 1997.

Rajhathy, Judit. *Free To Fly.* Halifax: New World Publishing, 1996.

Rapp, Doris. *Allergy and Your Family.* New York: Sterling Publishing Co., 1980.

Rapp, Doris. *Is This Your Child?* New York: Quill, William Morrow, 1991.

Shima, Mike. *The Medical I Ching.* Boulder: Blue Poppy Press, 1992.

Taylor, John. Helping Your Hyperactive Child. Prima Publishing and Communications, 1990.

Zong, Linda. *"Chinese Internal Medicine,"* lecture at SAMRA University, Los Angeles, CA. 1985

Case Histories from the Author's private practice,1984-present.

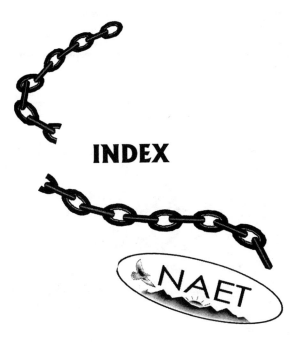

INDEX

Index

K

karaya gum 70
Kidney Meridian 120, 121
Kinesiology 23 74

L

Large intestine 107
Latex products 176
Lead 202
Learning disabilities. 235
Learning disorders 110
Lecithin 231
Life force 74
Like cures like 59
Liver meridian 129
Lung meridian 104

M

Macronutrients 220
Magnesium 194, 228
Malathion 209
Manganese 194, 229
Medication 65, 241
Mental confusion 110
Mercury 202
Meridians 75
Micronutrients 220
Milk 169, 185
Milk and calcium 185
Mind calming techniques 238
Mineral mix 170
MMR 207
Molds 46
Molybdenum 229
Mood swings, 32
MRT 18, 51. see also NAET
MRT to detect allergies 52

MSG 70, 201
Muscle Response Testing
51,86, 87

N

NAET 16, 71, 79. see also
western science
NAET Basic 15 groups 168.
Nambudripad's Testing Techniques 50.
Nasal congestion 104
Nausea 138
Nervous stomach 183
Nervousness 115
Neurotransmitters 77, 172, 202
Neutralizing technique 54
Night shade vegetables 176
Nitrates 201
Nor-adrenalin, 83
Nut mix 175
Nutrition 25
Nutritional supplements 221

O

Oriental medicine 24
Other hormones 174
Oval Ring Test 88

P

Panic attacks 183
Paper products 176
Parasite infestation, 33
PDM 89
Pediatric problems. 33
Penicillin 46
Perfume 174